The SERIAL KILLER'S APPRENTICE

ALSO BY JAMES RENNER

NONFICTION

Amy: My Search for Her Killer

FICTION

The Man from Primrose Lane

The SERIAL KILLER'S APPRENTICE

And 12 Other True Stories of
Cleveland's Most Intriguing
Unsolved Crimes

James Renner

GRAY & COMPANY, PUBLISHERS
CLEVELAND

Gray & Company, Publishers
www.grayco.com

Printed in the United States of America

ISBN 978-1-59851-046-1

For my dad, who always had my back.

Give me your blessing;
truth will come to light; murder cannot be hid long;
a man's son may, but in the end truth will out.

—Shakespeare, *The Merchant of Venice*

Contents

Foreword

---

by Robert Sackett

Captain in charge of the Beverly Jarosz case

Veteran homicide detectives have a rule of thumb: investigate quickly because the trail goes cold after 48 hours. In fact, a current popular television series is based on this premise. So why do police departments devote resources to cases that are 48 months or even 48 years old? And what part does the media and public's seemingly insatiable appetite for reading about these intriguing cases play in the process?

The practical reasons for reopening a case that has been dormant for years are well known. Murder has no statute of limitations, witnesses that were once reluctant to talk may come forward, accomplices may need to make a deal, and a murderer should never be allowed to think that he got away with it. Every generation has seen technological advances that give modern investigators the tools to solve a case that could not have been imagined by the original detectives. These are the reasons a cold case is solved; however, they do not explain why a detective presses on despite conventional wisdom and countless dead ends. Regardless of his claimed objective detachment, there is a human side that is the motivation for the investigators' dogged pursuit of "the answer."

After reading the files, you seek out family, friends, witnesses, retired officers, and anyone else who may give you some insight. You soon come to realize that the victim is not the only victim and you see and hear first hand how the crime has impacted so many lives for so many years. You realize the family has persevered in spite of the fact that they can never put this behind them and move on; it gets personal and you make a silent vow to make an arrest if it's the last thing you do. The original investigators did everything right, yet somehow you are determined not to let the family down a second time.

In words that are nearly sacrilegious in law enforcement circles, the media can be your best friend and play a crucial role in cold case investigations. Historically, the police release as little information as possible so not to compromise the investigation, yet the media naturally want all the details. These competing interests have created an adversarial relationship, even a distrust that must be set aside. Media involvement in cold cases generates the interest that may cause previously unknown persons to come forward with new information. There is also a negative side to publicity. In high profile cases, it seems that everybody has a theory and most cannot wait to talk about it. Suspects ruled out years ago, details so vague that they could not have been checked out at the time, not to mention years later, and conspiracy theories are all the subject of numerous calls. Nonetheless, cooperation with the media can be the impetus that uncovers the nugget that will later be called a breakthrough.

In the year 2038 when Detective Emily Smith of the Cuyahoga Regional Police Department is assigned an unsolved 2008 homicide case, no one can predict the technology that will be available to her. What is predictable is that she will work with the next James Renner and he will write a story so compelling that thousands will read it and it may generate the call that gives a family a long awaited answer and allows Detective Smith a well deserved good night's sleep.

Preface

On Writing True Crime

Sometimes I hunt killers. You could call it a hobby. Or maybe an obsession.

It's fun. It thrills me. It gives me focus. There's nothing quite like showing up on the doorstep of a suspect who has been hiding for decades and asking him directly if he committed murder. Knowing that they are the focus of a police investigation doesn't seem to mean much to these anonymous demons. But realizing that their name is going to appear in the newspaper always makes an impression.

Mostly, the crime stories I write about are unsolved homicides committed not by serial killers but by someone who has never murdered again. They don't follow patterns. There is no M.O. They are crimes of opportunity, in which the universe and dumb luck lined up in just the right way as to afford their killer the once-in-a-lifetime chance to kill and not get caught. Somehow, I'm more troubled by these random crimes; they suggest that many people are capable of committing murder if presented with the chance. These people then go about the rest of their lives as if nothing happened. Serial killers are a little easier to understand. They can't help it. And they'll go on killing until they get caught.

There's one killer in particular that I'm looking for: the guy who murdered Amy Mihaljevic in October 1989. I was just a few months older than Amy when she was murdered. I realized then that it could easily have been me who was taken. If a young girl could be kidnapped across the street from the Bay Village police department in broad daylight, the world was not the safe place our parents pretended it was. At 11 years old, I vowed to find Amy's killer one day. It is the primary reason I became a journalist.

Every time I research another unsolved homicide in Northeast Ohio, I'm also searching for anything that matches the Mihaljevic crime. I look for names of men who might have been questioned regarding Amy's murder. Every time I interview a suspect in another case, I ask him if he's ever lived in Bay Village.

I believe the man who killed Amy killed again. And if I can't find his name in the boxes of material I keep related to her case, maybe I'll find him while investigating some other girl's murder. Maybe I've met him already.

The most frustrating thing about Amy's case, and about the other unsolved cases you'll read about here (including tales of bank heists, false identities, and people who simply vanish into thin air), is the lack of answers, of justice. These are great mystery stories from which some jerk has ripped out the last chapter. Sometimes we can guess "who done it." But without that missing evidence or admission, without that last piece of the puzzle, we might never get to read a better ending. All I can say is, I tried to solve each and every one. I think I found the solution to a couple, though you're welcome to disagree with my conclusions. Maybe you can solve one yourself, based on the clues provided in these pages.

The good news is, in each case, there are still detectives devoted to giving us all the resolutions we hope for.

While researching these stories, I got to meet some of the area's finest police detectives and FBI agents. They take these cases home with them; this is not a nine-to-five job for any of them. And it's no fault of theirs that these cases remain unsolved. Life is not *CSI*. Killers don't always leave behind DNA and calling cards.

I don't know when we started to disrespect law enforcement as a general rule. Once upon a time, every kid in the neighborhood smiled when they saw a patrolman making his way across town and waved at him in his cruiser as he passed by. That doesn't happen much anymore. Witnesses don't want to talk to police because they are more concerned about what might happen to them if they "snitch" than they are about bringing the murderer to justice. Or maybe they're worried that once the police have their name, they'll be busted for something themselves. My generation avoids the cops. We turn the corner when we see them coming and call them pigs under our breath. We look out for Number One because we live in a state of constant fear, fueled in part by the media and our government. All we can think to do is keep ourselves safe. But, as any good detective will tell you, fear is mostly pointless.

The most common question people ask me when I talk about these crimes is, "Aren't you worried that the killer will track you down and kill you?"

The answer is, no. They never do, except on *CSI*. These guys are cowards, hiding in plain sight, without the emotional strength to take responsibility for what they have done. Especially the ones who pick on kids. They deserve to live in fear.

I hope you become as fascinated as I am by these unsolved mysteries. And if you think you've figured one out, please drop me line: jamesrenner@grayco.com.

The SERIAL KILLER'S APPRENTICE

CHAPTER 1

Dream a Little Dream of Me

The Unsolved Murder of Joseph Kupchik

In dreams, Joseph Kupchik never remembers that he's dead. Seems unaware that he plunged to his death off a parking deck in downtown Cleveland in 2006. It's always up to his twin brother, Johnathan, to give him the bad news.

John's dreams started shortly after Joe died and haven't let up since. Sometimes the two of them are at home, playing video games. In this one, they're shooting hoops. Joe bounces the basketball against the backboard, into the net, then returns it to his brother.

Joe, you're dead, says John. *You died.*

But Joe only stares at him, uncomprehending.

He's confused, John thinks. Or maybe I'm the one who's confused. Maybe this is real.

It's not, of course.

Joe is dead in the Real World.

The cops think Joe committed suicide. But if it was suicide, he found an unusual way to do it. A growing number of friends and family believe Joe was murdered.

Either way, when John wakes up, he'll have to leave Joe behind. So let's give them a moment alone. They've got a game to finish just now.

•   •   •

Joe and John Kupchik were hard to tell apart. Both inherited their mother's deep, dark eyes and their father's coarse, burgundy-brown hair. They had the same smile and gently sloping shoulders. Joe was slightly taller and had a larger nose and tilted his head when he met someone, almost bashfully. But they looked enough alike that John is reminded of Joe every time he looks in the mirror. He misses his twin and sometimes feels him, like an amputated limb. Their connection, that odd closeness that their sister Kate calls "the creepy twin thing," is still being severed.

The bets were small at first. Then Joe began laying down more money and losing more often than not.

The Kupchiks live in a modest two-story home inside a nondescript subdivision in Strongsville, domiciles of the shrinking middle class. Joe— "Kuppy" to friends—graduated from Strongsville High School in 2004. He wasn't much of an athlete; couldn't make a lay-up to save his life, friends say. But he played games of pick-up football in the neighborhood and loved watching the NFL on weekends, Green Bay in particular. He often wore a giant cheese head in the living room, though it's long been suspected he chose the team for its colors. Sometimes he made minor bets—a dollar or two—with John or his older brother Michael.

In the fall of 2004, then-18-year-old Joe and John decided it was time to discover their own destinies. John set off for the University of Dayton. Joe stayed home and enrolled at Cuyahoga Community College, taking accounting classes at the main branch in Parma.

During this time, Joe met many of his closest friends while working at Wendy's on Pearl Road. Joe was a crew leader and opened the store on Saturday and Sunday mornings. Megan Rachow, who still works at Wendy's, remembers Joe's knack for making endless shifts a little more entertaining. During lulls they played tic-tac-toe on the parking lot with chalk. Sometimes Joe put sandwich buns in the fryer. In retaliation for some prank she can no longer remember, Megan once put a ladle of cheese sauce in Joe's hat, but he noticed before putting it on. Out back one day, she offered him his first ciga-

Joseph Kupchik had recently lost money gambling, but friends and family owed him a lot more. And he showed no signs of depression. *(George Kupchik)*

rette, the single puff coming out in loud coughs a moment later as he laughed and laughed.

That first year at Tri-C, Joe pulled a C average. He figured his shifts at Wendy's were impacting his studies, so he quit in the fall of 2005. His transcripts show an immediate improvement. That semester, Joe took a full course load and earned two As and three Bs. He also became treasurer of the Tri-C Philosophy Club. Around this same time, he discovered online gambling.

The bets were small at first. He and John anted up $35 apiece to start an account at BoDog.com to bet on NFL games. They schemed over the phone and usually picked at least four winners for every seven games. By Christmas, their initial investment of $70 had ballooned to nearly $1,600.

Then Joe began betting on college basketball on their account, laying down more money and losing more often than not. When

Joseph and his brother Johnathan are twins whose bond cannot be severed, even after death. *(George Kupchik)*

John complained, Joe gave him half their winnings—about $800— and changed the password.

During the long winter break from school, Joe also started a new job at Steak 'n Shake in nearby Brunswick. He worked the grill at first and then began to wait tables. A co-worker recalls that Joe charmed many of his regular customers but had a hard time fitting in with other employees. They picked on him for bobbing his head when he talked, a nervous habit. And for talking too smart. Joe complained to a close friend that co-workers often changed his schedule, giving him less profitable shifts. (According to a former manager of the Brunswick Steak 'n Shake, employees were allowed to change the schedule as long as *someone* showed up.) All Joe's parents knew was that before leaving for work, he always left a note with his hours on the kitchen counter.

The morning of February 11, a Saturday, Joe's father, George, gathered receipts and W-2s for the family's tax filings. He also planned to fill out student loan paperwork, so that Joe could transfer to the University of Cincinnati later that year. While Joe was still in bed, George stuck his head inside his son's room.

"How much money do you have in your bank account?" George asked, waking him up.

"Seven thousand dollars," Joe replied.

After talking to his dad, Joe got up and dressed for work—black pants and a white button-up shirt. Before he left, Joe jotted down his work schedule for the day: noon to 10 P.M. George heard Joe shut the door of his Honda Civic. The sound echoes in George's mind still: the last noise he ever heard his son make. It was a little after 11 in the morning.

Only later would George learn that Joe had lied about his savings account. Some of the money had been loaned out to family and friends, but a lot had gone toward online bets. That morning, Joe's balance was $4.46.

Adam Worner, age 22, left the Blind Pig on West 6th that Saturday night around 1 A.M. and began the long walk back to his apartment on the east side of downtown Cleveland. His path lead him down Ontario Street. As he passed Fat Fish Blue, he came upon the body of a young man lying on the cement, just inside a thin alley, below a nine-story parking deck. He wasn't the first one on the scene. Later, he would say that he saw a black man, about his age, dressed in jeans and a nice jacket, standing over the body.

"I don't want to get into the blood and guts and gore of it," Worner says. He'll only say that the body belonged to a young man. That he was a bloodied wreck and unconscious, but not dead. That he was not wearing shoes. Worner used his cell phone to dial 911.

Sometime during the frenzy of activity as the EMS crew arrived and loaded the body into the ambulance, the black man quietly walked away. Worner is not sure he could recognize him if he saw him again on the street.

Officer James Foley arrived at the scene first and searched the garage. On the top floor, he found a Honda Civic with its driver's side door open, the keys dangling from the ignition, the engine turned off. The driver's seat was bloody, and a rolled-up white shirt covered in blood lay between the seat and the door, beside a bloody leather jacket. A pair of shoes rested on the floor under the steering wheel. A trail of blood snaked from the door to the railing. A six-inch fillet knife lay on the snowy cement a few feet from the car. Written on a piece of paper on the dash was Joseph Kupchik's phone number and home address. (George later recognized the handwriting as his son's.)

At 1:47 A.M., Joe arrived at MetroHealth Medical Center. EMS had placed him in a backboard and neck brace and had him hooked up to a ventilator. ER doctors discovered myriad injuries: broken ankles, a shattered pelvis, internal bleeding, and a punctured lung, the result of a stab wound in the left side of the chest, just below the collarbone. They tried to save him, but the damage was too extensive. Joe was pronounced dead at 3:08 A.M.

About seven hours passed before the Kupchiks learned any of this. As they arrived home from church at 10:30 A.M., police and media showed up simultaneously. Within minutes of the parents' learning that their son was dead, Channel 5 was at the door seeking an interview. The family shut the reporters out to grieve alone, but the media smelled a mystery and weren't about to forget it.

Dr. Frank Miller III, a pathologist for Cuyahoga County who was later appointed coroner, performed the autopsy on Joe's body. There were some strange details, for sure. Take that stab wound below Joe's left collarbone. Dr. Miller discovered the wound was quite deep, and that the knife had traveled front to back, downward, and left to right. That's Joe's left and right. So it didn't come in straight, but at an angle, pointing down and toward Joe's right side.

The other serious injuries were confined to Joe's lower body. His skull was not busted and his teeth were not broken, even though he is presumed to have fallen nine stories—Dr. Miller maintains his injuries were consistent with a fall from that height. It appeared that Joe had landed feet first—both ankles, both legs, and four ribs were fractured.

Miller also noted marks on Joe's stomach that looked like small cuts. There was no food in Joe's stomach, just a small amount of a

The crime scene. It's nine stories to the ground from the top level of the parking garage where detectives found Kupchik's car. *(Cuyahoga County Coroner's Office)*

red-brown liquid. Most likely, it had been several hours since he'd eaten. The red-brown liquid was never identified.

Joe's clothes were examined, too. His socks were clean, but his pants were caked with a white substance that turned out to be calcium sulfate, a compound found in de-icing material. His t-shirt, once white, was now mostly red and stiff with dried blood. It had been cut off during surgery and mended temporarily, like Joe, so that it could be photographed.

Cleveland Detectives Ignatius Sowa and James Gajowski were assigned to the case. They declined to be interviewed, but I managed to get my hands on a copy of their notes.

The detectives returned to the parking garage and got the video from the security camera that faces the entrance. Although they could not make out who was driving Joe's Honda when it pulled into the garage, the time on the video matched the time-stamped ticket discovered inside Joe's car: 1:04 P.M. Which means that the car was in the garage for over 12 hours before Joe's body was found on the street below. (The only thing they know about his travels between leaving home and entering the garage is that he stopped at the Wendy's on

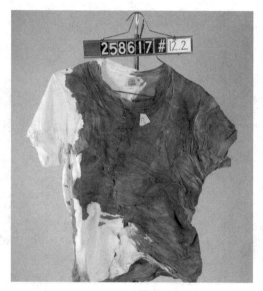

Joseph's bloody shirt was cut off of him at the hospital. It was too late to save him. Joseph couldn't tell doctors what had happened. *(Cuyahoga County Coroner's Office)*

Pearl Road where he'd once worked and ordered a chicken nugget meal at the drive-through.)

Near the space where the car was parked in the garage, the detectives found a pack of Newport cigarettes, two pens, and a beer bottle. On the street, they recovered Joe's belt buckle, which apparently had snapped off upon impact.

Sowa also noted that Joe had a roll of money tucked in his pocket: $103 (a ten, 5 fives and 68 singles). On the passenger seat they found Joe's book bag. Inside were two printed magazine articles, "Decisions About Death" and "The Harm That Religion Does." On the floor below was a textbook titled *Deviant Behavior*.

The detectives wondered what a preppy kid from Strongsville had been doing in a downtown parking garage for 12 hours. They wondered if it had something to do with the Ontario Café, a small bar next to Fat Fish Blue that turns queer after dark on weekends. They spoke to a regular twist known to frequent the club, but the man said he didn't know Joe.

Sowa and Gajowski interviewed co-workers at Steak 'n Shake. The schedule for the week of February 11 showed that Joe was supposed to come in at 5 P.M., not noon. So they spoke to the managers who had been on duty at 5 P.M. that day, Amber Cooper and Matt Magale, who told them because it wasn't a busy night, they decided not to call Joe's house when he didn't show up for work. One employee said Joe had appeared agitated during his Friday night shift and had forgotten to clock out.

Then the detectives learned the extent of Joe's gambling habit. In a two-day period in January, Joe had lost $1,800. It appeared he'd withdrawn money from Charter One after a significant loss to his BoDog account. The night before he died, Joe placed a $450 wager on college basketball.

They also reviewed the contents of the computer disks found in Joe's bag. Shortly before he died, Joe had written this passage:

> Expectations can either be positive or negative, but rarely am I ever right. Whenever I anticipate an event probably to make my dreams come true, something usually happens where the situation turns into a nightmare.

Adding this up with the gambling, the somber reading material, and the helpful note with name and address left in the car, the detectives informed the coroner's office of their conclusion: the kid had sat in his car for hours, stabbed himself, then jumped from the building. Suicide.

Dr. Miller has seen several cases in which people utilized multiple methods of suicide. There was the man who roped a noose around his neck before putting a shotgun in his mouth, for example. So he accepted the detectives' theory. Dr. Miller postulated that the scratches on Joe's stomach were probably "tick marks" where he'd tried to stab himself before finally getting the nerve to really push. He wrote up his own report for then–County Coroner Dr. Elizabeth Balraj.

Again, the media knew before the Kupchiks.

• • •

George Kupchik, Joe's father, is director of operations for a company that manufactures silicone sealants and greases. The job is as exciting as it sounds, but after years of analyzing data George's mind has become a finely tuned machine. When something isn't working at the factory, it's his job to find out why. He has learned from experience not to make rash decisions until he has reviewed all the evidence.

George was watching TV on May 22 when a local reporter for 19 Action News announced that his son's death would most likely be ruled a suicide.

George demanded a series of meetings with Dr. Balraj and her staff to convince them that his son was murdered before the ruling was made official. George presented Balraj and Miller with his own report on Joe's death, which he'd worked on during the Cleveland police investigation. He titled it *Questions and Facts about Joseph Kupchik*. There were many more questions than facts:

- Where is Joe's cell phone? (It should have been on him or in the car, but to this day it has not been found.)
- Why did Joe not call off from work if he didn't want to arouse suspicion?
- Where is the other man who found Joe's body and why didn't he stay to talk to police?
- With all the blood in the car (which George had to clean himself), would Joe have had enough strength to walk to the railing and climb over?
- If Joe was covered in blood, why was there no blood on the railing where he would have boosted himself up?
- Why would the police assume Joe was despondent over money, when relatives and friends owed him a combined $7,300 and he owned stock worth $4,000?
- If he was contemplating suicide, why did Joe place an online bet the night before—$450 on Georgetown to win the NCAA Tournament, which wasn't until March?
- Where did the knife come from? It didn't match any at home or from Steak 'n Shake.

- Could the right-handed Joe have inflicted that odd stab wound on himself? And speaking of wounds, couldn't those minor abrasions on his stomach have occurred when his belt snapped off upon impact?

George went on to note that Joe had been planning for his future. His grades at Tri-C were improving, and he'd just sent transcripts to the University of Cincinnati. He also explained that the *Deviant Behavior* textbook was required reading for a psychology class he was taking, and the articles found in his book bag and on the computer disk were for a philosophy class.

Dr. Balraj agreed there were enough unanswered questions to merit further investigation. She assigned two investigators from her own office, Alan Clark and Charles Teel. George knew that if the investigators could not prove reasonable doubt in Balraj's mind, his son's death would be forever labeled a suicide.

At the end of June, the Kupchiks were asked to return to the office of the county coroner. Dr. Balraj had settled on a ruling. The stakes were high not only for the Kupchiks, but also for Dr. Miller, whose reputation hinged on his own interpretation of the evidence.

Dr. Balraj informed George and Karen and Kate that Joe's death would be ruled "undetermined."

The Kupchiks were handed pictures of the crime scene, taken by detectives. Although the coroner was not ruling "suicide," she still believed the evidence supported the likelihood that Joe had taken his own life. The pictures were supposed to illustrate her point. Instead, it only confused the problem. One picture showed drops of blood inside a stairwell near where Joe's car had been parked.

"It was like, 'What the hell is this?'" Kate says, remembering the moment. She asked, "Is this Joe's blood? Has this been tested?"

The answer was no. According to Kate, Dr. Balraj took the photo and placed it next to her and exchanged a look with her protégé.

"I think she realized something hadn't been done," said Kate. "It was like, uh, yeah, you better test that."

Additionally, they learned that fresh vomit had been found on the stairwell, near the second floor.

Subsequent testing showed that the blood in the stairwell was from an unknown female. The vomit was not Joe's, either.

But the *Plain Dealer* seemed strangely reluctant to accept the new verdict.

"Apparent suicide can't be ruled as one" was the headline of the article the next day. The first paragraph read: "Joseph Kupchik killed himself but the coroner won't call it a suicide."

It was another blow to the Kupchiks, who were now convinced that Joe had been murdered. It would no longer be enough for them to prove Joe hadn't killed himself. Now, they had to find who did.

Joe hadn't worked at Steak 'n Shake long, but it was long enough to charm customer Fran Nagle. Fran is a loud-mouthed Italian with a Pittsburgh accent and a friendly spirit. She's hard to forget, and Joe would ask jokingly, "Would you like your usual table?" whenever she came in.

After Joe died, she thought about contacting the family. But when the June article appeared in the *Plain Dealer*, she decided to do more than that. She decided to get involved.

Fran met with Joe's mother, Karen, and the two formed a quick friendship. Fran knew how to work public records requests from the classes she had taken to earn a private investigator's license. She helped the Kupchiks gather evidence they needed to force the Cleveland police to take another look at the case.

One weekend, she and Karen drove out to the parking garage on Ontario to see what they could find. The two middle-aged women ascended the stairwell to the ninth floor but stopped short of opening the door. They heard a large group of people talking and music playing. "That place is party central on Saturday nights," says Fran.

They also noticed a large wooden container that garage employees use to store bags of salt to thaw ice and snow. The container was plenty big enough for a body and had a clasp that could be locked from the outside with something as simple as a pen. The inside walls

Apparent suicide can't be ruled as one

GABRIEL BAIRD
Plain Dealer Reporter

She ruled the manner of his
death "undetermined" but con-

Plain Dealer headline.

of the container were caked with white residue from bags of de-icing material. Fran wonders if it's the same residue that was caked on Joe's pants when they found him.

Later, Fran visited Steak 'n Shake and discovered something detectives had missed: Joe's schedule for February 11 had been altered. He'd been scheduled to work noon to 10 P.M., as he'd told his parents, but someone had changed it and no one could tell her by whom or when. The detectives had spoken only to evening managers, who would not have known about the change.

She also spoke to a Steak 'n Shake employee who had befriended Joe in the few weeks he worked there. Her name was Sarah Esper, a sprite of a girl with amber hair and a mischievous smile. She told Fran that Joe had talked to her about asking a girl from Tri-C out on a date for Valentine's Day, which would have been three days after his death.

When Sarah spoke to me in 2007, she remembered a little more. "Joe told me this girl had a boyfriend and that he didn't want the boyfriend to find out about their date," she says. "When he said that, he said it slyly."

Examining Joe's cell phone records, Fran noticed that in the days leading up to his death, Joe had called a friend named Tim Adams several times a day. Tim had called Joe's cell phone, too. It seemed like a day didn't go by without one calling the other. But on February 11, Joe didn't call Tim. And Tim never called Joe. It wasn't much, but it seemed odd.

She spoke to investigator Alan Clark about it, and according to Fran, Clark told her that he'd interviewed Tim, who'd claimed that his younger sister had told him a rumor about Joe: someone called

"J.C." supposedly knows what happened because he took Joe up to Cleveland, roughed him up, left his body some place, then came back later, stabbed him, and threw him off the building.

Tim told Clark he didn't know who J.C. was, but Tim's sister told Clark that J.C. was a friend of hers from Strongsville High School, and that the rumor was just a joke he had made in poor taste. Fran later learned something the girl apparently forgot to tell investigators: that J.C. had a twin brother whose first name also begins with J.

> **"I don't think Joe committed suicide. I think someone had to draw him down there."**

When George heard this, he was stunned. He had already called every number on Joe's last cell phone bill. One number he hadn't recognized rang into the voicemail of a man who called himself "J.C."

Tim Adams, a bright-eyed kid with spiky red hair, says that after his long-time girlfriend broke up with him, he started getting together with Joe. They would go skiing or see movies, mostly. Two days before Joe died, Tim says he lent Joe $500 to place an early bet for March Madness. George repaid Tim at the wake, after Tim asked about it.

"I don't think Joe committed suicide," says Tim. "I think someone had to draw him down there. I don't know if there was a basketball game that night, but if there was, maybe they lured him down for the game."

In fact, there was a Cavs game that night, against the Wizards. Tip-off was at 7:30.

Since 2006, the Kupchiks have tried to gain access to security camera footage recorded at the Cleveland garage where Joe's car was found from the afternoon and evening of his violent death. Key Bank owns the garage and the company's security team handles the cameras. When George first requested the tapes, he was assured, via e-mail, by Chief Security Officer James Biehl, that the video he requested would be copied and put someplace safe until they were able to get a subpoena from the courts that would allow Key Bank to legally release the footage to the family.

At the time, George felt that this was an easy out for Biehl, who he believes did not expect George to actually get a court order. But he did. In 2007, George contacted a close relative who works inside the Cleveland Police Department, who called in a favor, and in a blink Key Bank was served.

The tapes, Biehl told the family, had been lost.

After speaking to the Kupchiks and Fran Nagle, I attempted to get more information out of Joe's co-workers at the Brunswick Steak 'n Shake. Employees, however, had been instructed by managers on the day Joe's body was found not to speak to anyone about it, *especially* reporters.

Amber Cooper, who managed Steak 'n Shake the afternoon Joe disappeared, no longer works for the company. She claims the managers who would have seen Joe come in, if he did, were Tonya Walters and Brian Weaver.

When contacted, Walters said that "there's information that should be known" and promised to call back, but she never did. When reached again, she said that if she spoke to me, she would lose her job.

Brian Weaver, who now works at the Garfield Steak 'n Shake, was even less helpful. But he has reason to be wary of the media, who do better background checks than restaurant employers. Weaver has two felony convictions for stealing from the last company he worked for: Wendy's. While he was district manager for five area Wendy's restaurants, Weaver set up four "ghost employees" that he attached to the payroll, allowing him to cash bogus checks totaling more than $90,000. He was convicted in 2004. When Joe left Wendy's, Weaver was the manager who hired him at Steak 'n Shake.

Of course, Weaver wasn't the only manager with reason to avoid reporters asking questions about Joe. Matt Magale once tried to pressure Joe into joining a get-rich-quick scheme that promised financial independence by purchasing groceries online. Luckily, Joe didn't bite, but it soured their relationship.

Magale was eventually transferred out of the Brunswick Steak 'n Shake after a high school co-worker accused him of sexual harassment.

There was one more thing Cooper said. She claims a Steak 'n Shake employee named Bryan Trimmer was hanging out with Joe a lot right before his death.

Trimmer moved from Brunswick to Coupeville, Washington, not long after Joe was found dead. A Steak 'n Shake employee passed along a message from me to Trimmer and he called one night a little after 1 A.M. Trimmer confirmed that he and Joe had spent time together; they went to Applebee's once and sometimes drove around Medina in Joe's car. Sometimes he asked Joe to give him a ride to work or home afterwards. Trimmer also said he worked from 3 P.M. to midnight on February 11.

When asked if Joe came into Steak 'n Shake to work that day only to be sent home because they weren't busy, which is what some theorize, Trimmer said, "He didn't come in; he called. He wanted to change his schedule. Said it had something to do with school."

Joe's cell phone records show no evidence of this.

When asked why Joe would go downtown, Trimmer said, "What's the big deal? I go downtown all the time."

When asked if managers and other employees would confirm that he was, in fact, working when Joe was missing, Trimmer hedges. "I'm not 100 percent sure if I was working that day. But I can't remember what I had for breakfast yesterday."

Brunswick police currently have a warrant out for Trimmer's arrest for failing to appear in court on a misdemeanor charge of underage possession of alcohol.

Kate Kupchik sits at a table inside Caribou Coffee in Akron, sipping her drink and expounding on what may have happened to her brother nearly a year ago. She looks more like her mother than her other siblings, but has darker hair. There's a little bit of Joe in her, too, in the contours of her cheeks. And she has her father's analytical mind; she currently works as an accountant.

"I don't think anybody intended to kill Joe," she says. "I see it like this: they held a knife to him as a scare tactic and someone moved. Someone panicked. He was knocked unconscious. He was stored somewhere. They left and came back and then threw him off. Then said, 'Let's change his schedule to five so that we're gone by then and we'll be off the clock and off the hook.' Maybe they said, 'Here's $1,000 to change the schedule, just shut up about it.' Unfortunately, there's people out there that would take the money. I think everyone involved is young, which is a good thing. Maybe they had a girlfriend or boyfriend then who they told. Maybe now, they're broken up. And now, this ex will come forward and say, 'I know what happened.'"

On February 11, 2006, as the day faded into evening and a nearly full moon hung in the winter sky, John Kupchik attended a party at a friend's house near the University of Dayton. But he didn't feel right. In fact, he felt distraught for no apparent reason. He wondered if he was getting sick. He left early and went back to his dorm to lie down.

He had no idea that at that moment his twin brother was dying.

Their connection persists, through dreams. Maybe one day Joe can rest in peace and John can rest through the night.

Anyone with information related to Joe's case can give anonymous tips to Crimestoppers at 216-252-7463. You can also contact the family at HelpJoeK@ sbcglobal.net.

CHAPTER 2

Time is Death Itself

The Unsolved Murder of Beverly Jarosz

She knew that Death wanted her and in the months before her violent murder, 16-year-old Beverly Jarosz did everything she could to prepare for it.

She ruminated on the subject of death, the idea of it, in poems she kept in a small black book. "Someone will want to publish these when I'm dead," she told her little sister, Carol.

She studied ways of seeing her own future before it came to pass, reading books on parapsychology and palm reading.

She locked the doors when she got home from school every day. She made sure the curtains were snuggly shut before dark. And she bought an ornate letter opener—more of a knife, really—which she kept on the desk in her bedroom by the door that led downstairs, "just in case."

Her mother felt it, too. A dark foreboding. Danger, headed their way.

This sense that Beverly had fallen within the Reaper's regard began in the summer of 1964, around the time she received an anonymous present tucked into the back door of her family's house in Garfield Heights. It was a gift-wrapped box from Higbee's, tied up in a blue ribbon. Someone had written "To Bev" on the box. Inside was a silver bracelet and ring. She had no clue who had sent it. There were a lot of young men in the neighborhood who wanted to date her, after all. It could have been any one of them. But the anonymity of it frightened her.

By the end of '64, though, things were looking up. Beverly—Bev, as her friends called her—had started dating a strait-laced college boy, a young Republican named Roger McNamara. He was a far cry from her first love—the town bad boy, Dan Schulte. Roger was reserved, a proper Catholic who attended Latin mass and spoke out against the liberal alterations of Vatican II. Dan's idea of a date had been making out behind the local car wash. Bev's sister, who had never cared for Dan, liked Roger. He treated her well. Bev particularly enjoyed attending parties at Roger's fraternity and meeting his older, educated friends.

But this new happiness was short lived.

Death finally caught up with Bev on December 28, 1964.

The Jarosz (pronounced *Jar-rose*) family home was a modest two-story structure that sat on Thornton Avenue, near Turney, in suburban Garfield Heights. It was a cookie-cutter neighborhood of similar homes packed tightly together in neat little rows, separated by thin driveways and well-kept lawns. The residents were blue collar types, hard-working Clevelanders who pulled late shifts at the local factories and 9-to-5ers who arrived home at the end of the evening in swarms of American-made metal. Most women didn't work outside the home, and people really knew their neighbors and invited them to dinner. During the 1964 Christmas holiday, however, several men on Thornton were home more than usual because the union at White Motor Company was striking.

Bev's father, Ted, was the co-owner of a small lighting and manufacturing firm but had a real knack for woodworking. In his spare time, he built toys and chests. Over the course of a few years, he slowly renovated the entire second floor of his house, converting it into a shared bedroom for his two daughters. He constructed everything in duplicate so that neither felt slighted. Each had a wooden nook beside her bed to store little girl treasures. And each had a bookcase—on Bev's was the collected works of Edgar Allan Poe.

Beverly's school picture. In the months leading up to her murder, Beverly feared she was supposed to die. *(Garfield Heights High School yearbook)*

They had their own dressers and mirrors. Between their beds was a shared nightstand.

Bev's mom, Eleanor, worked in a local office. Bev's sister, Carol, was a seventh grader at St. Therese and had started taking horseback riding lessons. Usually, when Bev was asked out on a date, she asked Carol what she thought of the boy before she accepted. They were a close family, a family with no secrets.

Bev was a striking young woman with a nicely curvy figure and eyes the color of the lake on an overcast day. She preferred jazz to the Beatles, and she often visited the Cleveland Museum of Art, spending hours by herself, silently contemplating master works. She attended Marymount High, a private Catholic school, where she was a member of the Future Teachers club. She spoke Latin. She volunteered time at the local hospital. In the summers, she liked to sunbathe in the backyard and read books. By all accounts, she was exceedingly popular, intelligent, and well-liked.

Which made it all the more shocking that her murder was so hateful, so violent.

Carol later gave detectives a detailed account of her sister's last day.

"Monday, December 28, Bev and I got up about eight-thirty, nine o'clock. We had breakfast and then washed dishes from the night before."

The dishes were left over from a small gathering in the Jarosz home the previous evening. Their neighbors on both sides—the Webers and the Zumgulises—had come over for snacks and drinks. It was a Christmastime tradition. Bev had come in and out during the party, leaving briefly at the end of the night for a short car ride with her boyfriend.

After the dishes were done, the girls got dressed and left the house around 10:15 A.M. Bev wore slacks and a white blouse with a black cardigan. Carol walked with Bev first to Woolworth's to pick up a hairnet for their grandmother, then to Hough Bakery for some bread. At about 10:45, they arrived at Grandma Vanek's and ate lunch: ham sandwiches and coffee. Bev told Carol she was going to return home and meet up with a friend named Barb Klonowski at 12:30. Bev and Barb were going to visit another friend named Margie Gorney for the afternoon. Around 12:15, a young man named James Mondzelewski, who lived next door to Bev's grandmother, drove her home while Carol stayed with Grandma Vanek.

At 1 P.M., Bev called her mom at work. The call was brief. Bev said she had to go because Barb was supposed to be there any minute and she still needed to change.

Barb's mother dropped her off at the Jarosz house at 1:20 and left before Barb reached the side door. Barb saw that the storm door was closed but the inner door was open to the kitchen, which was strange, because Bev always kept both doors closed and locked. Inside the family room, the radio was blaring classical music from WCLV. Barb rang the doorbell three times but Bev didn't answer the door. She thought it was possible Bev couldn't hear the bell over the radio so she tried to open the glass storm door, but it seemed to be locked. Barb went around front.

The Jarosz home on Thornton Avenue in Garfield Heights. Beverly's killer fled through the back door. *(Garfield Heights Police Department)*

There she rang the front doorbell and this time she distinctly heard a sound from upstairs, like a dresser drawer being opened loudly. She figured Bev was getting dressed so she pulled a magazine from the mailbox beside the door and sat on the steps, reading for a few minutes. When Bev didn't come to the door after several more minutes, Barb wondered if Bev was mad at her for being late. So Barb gave up and started walking home again. Before she got too far, though, a young man named Gary Grayson offered her a ride in his '58 Corvair.

Back home, Barb tried to reach Bev on the phone, but no one answered. At around 3:45, Margie called Barb's house to see what was taking so long. When Barb told her that Bev had stood her up, Margie called Bev's grandmother to see if she was over there. When Grandma Vanek got no answer at the Jarosz home either, she called Bev's father at work.

Sensing something was wrong, Ted rushed home. He pulled into the driveway at 4:10 P.M.. There, he found the side storm door unlocked. The inner door was still open. The radio was still playing loudly inside. Upstairs, he discovered the lifeless body of his daughter lying face-down in a pool of blood on the floor beside her bed.

The crime scene: the bedroom Beverly shared with her younger sister. *(Garfield Heights Police Department)*

It was a horrific scene. Bev's blouse and bra were pulled up over her breasts. Her slacks and underwear had been yanked down in one single, forceful motion. Her backside was riddled with deep gashes—she had been stabbed over 40 times. Her left hand was tucked under her body and her right hand was at her neck, where she had received another deep stab wound. Above the bed, where the ceiling slanted low from the pitch of the roof, was a large hole in the plaster, possibly created as she kicked at her attacker during the struggle.

An autopsy determined that it wasn't the stab wounds that killed her, but rather the length of rope wrapped around her neck. She had been strangled to death by a piece of clothesline tied with a square knot. Her murderer had become so violent that he accidentally cut part of the rope as he stabbed her and a piece of it was still wrapped in her fingers.

During the initial investigation into the murder of Beverly Jarosz, every man in Garfield Heights was a potential suspect. It was tough work for investigators. As police canvassed the neighborhood, they found several young men who had taken Bev on dates and even more who had been rejected.

They questioned 21-year-old Bruce Bilek, a college student who lived directly behind Bev's house, after detectives discovered a note Bev had written to Margie: "Bruce came over to see what I looked like when I'm not dressed. I have my blue robe on and my hair is still in curlers." But Bilek denied ever really talking to Bev and he had a solid alibi—at the time of the murder he was home with his family, working on his car. And Margie told detectives that it wouldn't be unusual for Bev to make up the incident. Bev sometimes wrote about daring situations, Margie said, "because nothing ever happened to her."

> **During the initial investigation, every man in Garfield Heights was a potential suspect.**

Police also looked at Barb's cousin, Stanley Klonowski, who had once dated Bev until she broke it off. "I feel sorry for Stanley because he's so misunderstood, troubled, and disturbed," Bev had written. But that didn't pan out, either. They questioned Larry Young, whose mother had bad-mouthed Bev after the girl dumped her son. They looked closely at every male who had been seen at the house: the grocery-bagger at the local A&P, the boy in her typing class who gave her rides home, and countless other would-be suitors.

They interviewed 19-year-old John Paliyan, who lived two doors down from the Jarosz's. He was home alone the day of the murder and admitted eyeing Bev whenever she sunbathed in the back-yard.

And, of course, they spoke to James Mondzelewski, who had driven Bev home. He said the whole trip had lasted 15 minutes, after which he returned home, changed his clothes, and had a bite to eat. Later, he had driven Mrs. Vanek to the Jarosz home to be with the family after Bev's body was discovered. There was nothing in his character for police to question and he was quickly ruled out.

Slowly, the investigation narrowed to those closest to Bev.

After talking to family members, detectives took a look at Bev's former steady, Dan Schulte. He had dropped out of high school to join the Air Corps but was back in town for Christmas. And, although he was dating a new girl, it was well known that he still pined for Bev, to the chagrin of Bev's friends, who thought he was nothing but a bad influence. "She would never think of doing the things with Roger that she did with Dan," Margie told police. He had shown up at Bev's viewing with a girl at his side but had returned alone, later, and sat quietly by himself.

While on leave, Schulte had picked up some part-time work and was able to produce a timecard that showed he was on the clock when Bev was murdered. But the woman who lived next door to Schulte's home told police she had seen him come home that day and run inside in a hurry. She had watched him in the reflection of her garage window. So Schulte was given a lie-detector test, which he passed.

Roger McNamara's alibi was weak. He told investigators he had been home sick. He, too, was given a lie detector test, which he passed. But the next day, Detective William Horrigan told the *Cleveland Press*, "There are some elements to his present story that bother some of us."

While Horrigan questioned a growing list of suspects, other detectives gathered evidence from the crime scene. They lifted fingerprints from Bev's bedroom. Several were found that could not be matched to family or close friends. They also found bits of Bev's hair in a bush behind the house, indicating that the murderer had escaped via the back door. The one thing no one could find was the brass letter opener Bev kept in her room.

During the course of the autopsy, the coroner discovered that Bev had not been raped. In fact, she had never even had sex. Was it possible that her friend Barb had interrupted the attack when she rang the doorbell? Or was the scene staged to look like a sexual assault?

There was one other odd clue. Bev had apparently received a phone call when she was home alone the day of her murder. She had written a message for her father and placed it next to the phone.

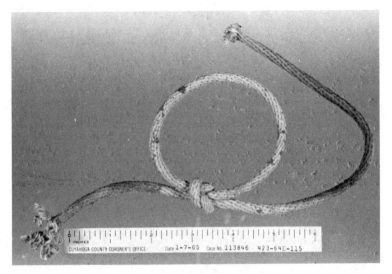

Beverly's killer stabbed her so violently that the rope being used to strangle her was accidentally cut. *(Cuyahoga County Coroner's Office)*

It read: "Stephen Stackowicz called. Will call back later." But her father didn't know anyone by that name. And Stackowicz never did call back. Detectives theorized it may have been the killer, calling to make sure Bev was home alone.

As the leads grew cold, police consulted a specialist who provided them a detailed profile of the killer's mind. "The killer may have been attracted to the girl by some feature that reminded him of his mother's face," the report said. "He has a fear of being rejected. The killer would justify the act to himself by believing the girl was making him feel sick and this was the only way to cure himself."

Reporters interviewed a middle-aged neighbor named James Krawczyk, who claimed to have seen the killer run away from the Jarosz house. He was home because of the White Motor strike, and his wife confirmed to journalists that he often stood by the window, looking out toward Bev's house on Thornton Avenue. "Sometimes, he even gets up at night to look out the window," she said. "I guess he likes the view." But Krawczyk later admitted to police he had made up the story to get his name in the paper

On January 11, as the local press demanded the killer be brought

Classmates at Marymount High mourned the loss of their friend.
(Cleveland State University, Cleveland Press Archives)

to justice, a 17-year-old boy from the neighborhood committed suicide. People quickly assumed he was responsible and had taken
his life because he was overwhelmed with guilt. But police found
the boy had been working at the time of the murder and several co-
workers backed up the timecard.

Eventually, the tips generated by the media coverage slowed to
a trickle. Garfield Heights detectives continued to follow every lead
until it dead-ended. They spent years on the case. It became personal to the homegrown investigators who devoted their time to
finding Bev's killer. But there was never enough evidence to charge
anyone with the crime, though detective Horrigan believed he knew
who did it. "I had who I was convinced was the killer the second day
after the murder," he told a *Plain Dealer* reporter in 1989. "He passed
several interrogations. I hope one day he'll blow his top and talk."

That hasn't happened yet.

Garfield Heights has not changed significantly in 43 years. It's
still a blue-collar town, though most of the factories that once employed its residents have either closed or moved to warmer climes.
Serious crimes have risen steadily over the years as the city moved

closer and closer to the suburb, but south of Miles Road, it's still safe enough to walk to the store or bike to a friend's house. Thornton Avenue still looks the same. The houses and lawns are still well-maintained, though they look *smaller*, somehow. And inside the Raymond Stackowicz Justice Center, Garfield Heights detectives are working the Beverly Jarosz case again.

This time around, the investigation is being lead by Captain Robert Sackett and Detective Carl Biegacki, two men who grew up in Garfield Heights and who understand the community intimately. Captain Sackett is friendly and quick to smile, a wiry man who likes his job and wants to tell you so, but not in so many words. Above his desk is a handcrafted wooden train, made by Ted Jarosz. Detective Biegacki ("common spelling," he jokes) is more stoic, with a dry sense of humor but a similar affection for his tough occupation. The pair reopened the Jarosz case in 2004, hoping that advances in DNA might yield new clues. They asked "six or seven" people to submit DNA and requested the coroner's office test evidence for the presence of DNA as well. They pored through the old case files and newspaper clippings, searching for the smallest detail that might unlock the riddle. And even though they do not know, for sure, the identity of Bev's killer, they have come to understand him well through the facts of the crime.

"A girl didn't do this," says Sackett.

"This was a blitz-style attack on her," says Biegacki. "He definitely came from behind with the rope, which was prepared before he got there."

"We think it is someone she knew," Sackett continues. "There wasn't a struggle on the first floor. All the violence is upstairs, which leads you to believe she let this person into the house. But what's this guy's real intent? Was it rape or was it murder?"

"Why did he bring two weapons?" asks Biegacki, meaning the rope and whatever instrument he used to stab her 40 times. It's unusual for someone to bring two murder weapons to a crime scene.

Quickly, their passion for solving this case and their frustration from not yet having done so becomes evident. They could theorize forever about intent, but it brings them no closer to a resolution.

(Cleveland State University Archives)

Detective Horrigan spent most of his life hoping for a resolution that never came. It must have been even harder for him.

"I know how not solving this makes me feel," says Sackett, shaking his head.

"It drives you crazy," says Biegacki. "But you can only do your best with what you have on your desk."

While researching this story, I was given permission to view documents at the coroner's office that were collected by investigators in 1964. From those papers I was able to gather the names of several people who were questioned about the crime. One person I contacted was John Paliyan, the young man who had once lived two doors east of the Jarosz residence. Paliyan was asked to take a lie detector test in 1965, but the results were inconclusive. A man who worked with Paliyan at that time claimed Paliyan asked him how to beat the test.

Paliyan surprised me by saying any request for an interview should go through his lawyer, Jay Milano. Apparently, he had recently spoken to detectives from Garfield Heights. He claimed he was being framed and that there was a cover-up going on. He is currently dying of lung disease but was smoking a thin cigar when I dropped by his house one afternoon. Paliyan also said his sister had been questioned and so I visited her as well.

Paliyan's sister did not talk to me, but her husband did. He's still angry that Garfield Heights detectives visited his wife at work and interrogated her for over an hour before putting her in a cruiser to take her to the station for more questioning. According to him, the detectives wanted to know if she had disposed of the murder weapon for her brother. But his wife contacted an attorney on her cell phone on the way to the station, and on the advice of that lawyer, asked to be dropped off before they got to Garfield Heights.

> *"I think about her every day. I have no one to remember my childhood with."*

"It's nonsense," says the husband. "And we would have cooperated with police if they had treated her kindly."

Sackett and Biegacki won't comment on any specific suspect. They will only say that there are a number of men they keep an eye on.

Roger McNamara still lives in Northeast Ohio and has worked for a number of financial firms over the years. He remains a steadfast Republican and Catholic. I caught up with him as he was leaving his apartment for a short walk one evening, with a cigarette in one hand and a cup of coffee in the other. He declined an interview. Dan Schulte could not be located. He left the country in 2005 and is rumored to be living in Israel.

"It was somebody close," says Biegacki. "If you start taking 10 steps outside the box, you get lost. It's usually a simple answer. Look, prosecution is not the main goal for the family. Before Bev's parents pass they would just like to know what happened. God may forgive you, but the family still deserves to know."

The Jarosz family also still hopes for closure.

"I think about her every day," says Carol. "I have nobody to remember my childhood with. No nieces or nephews to share my children's lives with. I think about her all the time. I had a dream about her the other night. We were walking together near Canton and I lost her. I thought, 'I'll never see her again.' But then I turned the corner and there she was."

"I've only dreamt about her once in all these years," says Bev's mother, Eleanor. "In the dream, she was living upstairs in Grandma's house and I was so happy to see her. I dream about other people all the time, but never her."

Carol still has Bev's book of poems and keeps it nearby like a talisman. One of the last entries is dated July 17, 1964:

> *What is this thing called time?*
> *Time is measured eternity.*
> *It is that which is counted*
> *between the meetings of foolish lovers.*
> *Time is a wilted flower . . .*
> *or a dead bird.*
> *It is a graying half moon*
> *in a midnight sky.*
> *Time is death itself.*

Anyone with information related to this crime can contact Garfield Heights police at 216-475-3056.

CHAPTER 3

The River's Edge

The Unsolved Disappearance of Ray Gricar

The village of Bellefonte—which the residents pronounce *Bell-font*—is located alongside a river on the side of a mountain in central Pennsylvania. In the fall months, the town is saturated with hues of red, brown, and yellow from leaves hanging from the maples, oaks, and elms of the endless forest that surrounds it.

The tale of Ray Gricar's disappearance is already legend here.

Plaza Centre Antiques is in sight of the courthouse where Gricar worked. Two gray-hairs biding time at a card table near the entrance are happy to share their theories on the fate of the prosecutor.

"Someone got rid of him," says Karl Rudeen, the one in the blue cap. "Everyone he put in jail has a motive. Take a number, get in line. He was killed for what was on that computer."

"Now hold on," interjects Ron Denker, a skinny fellow in a red flannel button-down, his white hair slicked back against his skull. "The man took an early vacation. Started a new life somewhere. I've thought about doing it. Everyone has. And he knew how to do it, because that was his business."

The two men bicker and change their minds. Finally, they give up, frustrated. Denker walks away to tend to his section of the store.

"We've had a couple guys disappear around here, never seen again," Rudeen says in a low voice. "But that's just from a couple of wags." He shrugs. "Maybe he'll show up downstream, in Yellow-knife."

.   .   .

Visitors to Bellefonte stay at Schnitzel's Tavern, a historic brick hotel constructed in 1868, one of the first in the country to have electric lights. Today, it advertises "Authentic German Dining in an Old World Setting." Across the street, a tall monument honors the seven men from Bellefonte who went on to become governor. Orange koi swim under a bridge in the park and for a quarter you can feed them.

At the center of town, High Street splits in two at a memorial for soldiers killed in combat and loops around the county courthouse and jail. Until 2005, the man in charge there was District Attorney Ray Gricar. Gricar was a Cleveland kid. Collinwood native, avid Indians fan.

Off Lamb Street is a large brick building, mostly garage, which serves as both the police station and firehouse. More than 30 bicycles lean against a wall beside two cruisers, just inside the back door. "You'd be surprised how many people lose a bike and never come to claim it," says Officer Darrel Zaccagni (pronounced *Zeg-anny*) as he leads me upstairs. You can tell this bit of information digs at him a little, a collection of stories without conclusion.

On the second floor, a conference room serves as both the city council chambers and a fine place to interview witnesses. The room has a sterile, cold feeling, drab walls contrasting with the tall-backed red leather chairs that surround a cheap wooden table. The officer sits and sighs. He was supposed to meet with Fox News today about the Gricar case, but they canceled again. They keep bumping him for updates on Michael Jackson, Natalee Holloway, hurricanes, the horror of the moment. His uniform is still crisp for the canceled interview.

He wrings his hands, considering where to start.

"His girlfriend called us 11, 11:30, that night to report Ray had not come home yet," he begins.

"Wait," I ask. "Take it from the beginning. How did you know Ray? Can you tell me a little about him?"

"Ray was the district attorney—county prosecutor, same thing

Ray Gricar was about to retire as District Attorney when he vanished. *(Bellefonte Police Department)*

out here—for 20 years. I would go to his office sometimes and talk to him about a case. He was the type of guy where when we were done [talking], he would go over and open the door and wait for me to leave. You didn't chitchat with Ray at work. He would walk right by you in the hallway. He would just be so focused. When you went into the office, if you didn't know there was a relationship between them, you couldn't tell."

"Between Ray and Patty, his girlfriend?"

Zaccagni nods. Patty Fornicola worked in the prosecutor's office as a victims' rights advocate. They started dating after Gricar's second marriage dissolved. Zaccagni has known her since she was in high school and he was a rookie.

Pity the small town officer who finds himself swallowed up by high-profile mystery. With this one, it's tempting to rush past the beginning and jump ahead like this, to the laptop the fishermen found in the river, to the possible sighting in Texas, and work the clues backward. That seems the easiest way to go. Taken chronologically, it's easy to get lost.

·   ·   ·

The life of Ray Gricar never diverged much. It was as if a path had been set for him at birth, which he followed obediently for 59 years.

Ray was born in October 1945, in the first wave of the Baby Boom. His family lived in the proudly Polish section of Collinwood. Growing up, Ray became passionate about Cleveland sports and often went to Indians games with his older brother, Roy. Later, he attended Gilmour Academy, an expensive Catholic preparatory school in Gates Mills, and earned a bachelor's degree from the University of Dayton, where he met a young freshman named Barbara Gray.

Though he first had aspirations to study Russian history, he focused on law after landing an internship at the prosecutor's office. After graduation, he and Barbara moved to Cleveland and married in 1969. He earned a law degree from Case Western Reserve University and took a job as an assistant prosecutor for Cuyahoga County. He went after career criminals. Rape. Murder. The tough cases.

In 1978, he and Barbara adopted a newborn girl, Lara. When Barbara was offered a position at Penn State in 1985, Ray took some time off, opting to become a stay-at-home dad. They moved into a house near State College, Pennsylvania. This brief respite from the dark side of human nature was short-lived. Eventually, the darkness found him.

Word in Bellefonte was a young prosecutor had moved to Centre County, looking to get away from the big city. It just so happened that District Attorney David Grine needed a part-time assistant. It doesn't appear that Gricar put up much of a fight when the town posse came knocking at his door. Maybe he thought this would be different. After all, Centre County sees only one or two homicides a year.

Gricar became first assistant prosecutor for Centre County in 1985. When the D.A. became a judge later that same year, Gricar ran for the open position, and won.

Even though the D.A. gig was considered part-time, he often put in over 40 hours a week. That first year, he successfully prosecuted one of the first cases in the country to use postpartum depression as a defense after a woman tossed her one-month-old son from a bridge

MISSING
PERSON

April 15, 2005
Bellefonte, Pennsylvania

RAY FRANK GRICAR

Detectives are still searching for Gricar. Have you seen him? *(www.FBI.gov)*

into a local stream. She got 8 to 20 years. In 1992, he prosecuted James R. Cruz, an interstate trucker who had dumped the body of a young girl on the on-ramp to I-80 heading out of town. Cruz was found guilty and sentenced to life in prison. When an ROTC student opened fire in the student union at Penn State in 1996—killing one girl and wounding another—Gricar put the shooter away for 30 to 60 years. Homicides were his specialty.

He and his wife divorced in the early '90s, but it appears the only other time Gricar's life took an unexpected turn was in May 1996, when his brother, Roy, suddenly disappeared. Roy was living in Dayton at the time. He had just been fired from his job as a private contractor at Wright Patterson Air Force Base. He suffered from bipolar disorder and had been acting erratic. On the pretense of heading to the store to buy a bag of mulch, Roy left the house and didn't come back.

For the next week, Tony, Roy's son, searched for his father. Ray drove to Dayton to speak to the local police and media. Then, Roy's body was found in the Great Miami River. Cause of death was determined to be suicide by drowning.

Tony says his uncle was noticeably affected by the tragedy. But the always-focused Ray tried his best to move forward. A month later he married his second wife, Emma. While Gricar was withdrawn, Emma was social and outgoing. She liked to dance. Maybe he liked her for the way she complemented his silent nature. But in the end, the differences were too great. They divorced in 2001.

"There are enough clues to take you in any direction. And enough left over to rein you back in."

In January of 2005, after two decades as district attorney, Gricar announced he would not seek reelection. He wanted to travel, he said. He wanted to visit his daughter, Lara, in Seattle, where she attended college, maybe spend some time in New England—he especially liked Vermont.

On Friday, April 15, Gricar told his new girlfriend, Patty Fornicola, he wouldn't be going to work that day. He said he was going to play hooky and head into Lewisburg, an hour's drive to the east, to do some antiquing. This was not unusual. Gricar would often take a half day off to visit antique shops in nearby towns, questing for vintage toys. Small metal cars. Outdated appliances.

Fornicola asked him to call if he wouldn't be back in time to walk the dog at noon. That was the last time she saw him.

Since then, Tony has found himself filling the role for his uncle that Ray once took for Roy: family spokesman. The 32-year-old entrepreneur from Dayton now lives in seclusion at a family-owned condo in Celina, Ohio. He ventures out for Penn State games and to track down fresh leads in his uncle's case. The lack of resolution wears on him.

"There are enough clues to take you in any direction," he says. "And enough left over to rein you back in."

Officer Darrel Zaccagni's voice takes on the air of urgency as he gets to the meat of his story, the part where Ray Gricar stops being an aloof acquaintance and becomes the main focus of his job.

Zaccagni begins: "He called [Fornicola] about 11:30 that morning

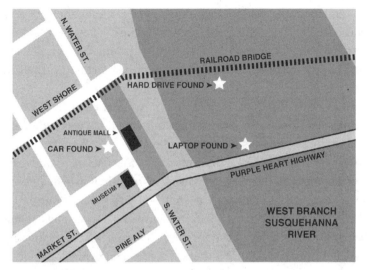

Gricar was last seen here, in Lewisburg, Pa. The clues he left behind defy the laws of physics. *(Ron Kretsch)*

and said, 'Well, I'm on 192. I'm not going to make it home in time to take care of the dog.' He says, 'See you later.'" Fornicola recalls nothing usual about his tone.

"When he wasn't home at dinner time—she kind of expected him home by then—and when he wasn't there, she thought, 'What's keeping him? Oh, he stopped to get something to eat.' But when it got to be ten, eleven o'clock at night, she's like, 'No, he should be home by now.' So then she called us.

"We put out a local message to be on the lookout for him. In the morning, we started taking it a little more seriously. Obviously, this was now a missing person."

That Saturday evening, a state trooper spotted Ray's car in a parking lot across from an antique mall in Lewisburg. The interior and exterior of the car were examined, the surrounding area searched. There were no signs of a struggle, and no one had attempted to wipe away fingerprints.

"The biggest thing that was found in that car that didn't jive with what we know about Ray was some cigarette ashes," Zaccagni continues. "Now, we're not talking a lot. But some minute cigarette ash on the passenger's side. When they opened the car, they got a to-bacco smell. A cigarette smell came out of the car. Ray didn't smoke. And he never let anybody smoke inside his Mini Cooper. Ray was very fastidious about his car. The cell phone was in there, turned off. Nothing appeared to be missing.

"Later, we went to the house and his work and collected all the computers he used for processing. [To] see if there was something on his computers to tell us what had happened. When we went to collect the computer from the house, Patty asked us if we wanted his work laptop, too. They had been using his work laptop to do Internet searches and things, but had recently bought a separate one for the home. 'So we don't use it anymore,' Patty said. So she goes up and brings down the empty case and says, 'It's not here.' So, it's missing, but all the peripheral stuff is there: the power cord, the floppy drive, everything extra you would need for the laptop. It's all there. The only thing missing is the laptop with its self-powered battery that lasts for two or three hours.

"The question becomes, why would a person who's just going for a leisurely drive take the time to go upstairs and remove the laptop from its case and take it with them? Why not take the case?"

Zaccagni anticipates my response. *This makes no sense.*

"It makes a lot of sense," he replies with a smile, before returning to the chronology.

"Friday night, people remember the car sitting in the parking lot. It's a very distinct car. Two people in the antique mall are positive they saw him in there. One man is positive he saw Gricar talking to a female on several occasions. I asked him, Were they together? He said, 'Well, in my mind they were together, but they weren't holding hands; they weren't lovey-dovey or anything.'

"We have three or four good witnesses from down there who are definitely ID-ing him in the park. They saw him sitting in his car. They watched him driving his Mini Cooper back and forth on Fri-day.

"We can definitely put him there on Saturday, too. There's a mu-seum right here, across from the park. I think it's called Cottingwood House. The employees there watched Ray bring his car and park it two or three different times across the street. He came and left, came and left, came back. He got out of his car, sat on a bench. He was reading a newspaper or something. But by noon Saturday, he just seems to have fallen off the earth."

What does Zaccagni make of all this?

"Depends on what theory you want to go after," he says, pulling himself up to the table. "You have three prominent theories here."

Theory one: homicide. Twenty years spent convicting Centre County's most hardened criminals earns you some enemies. Maybe some thug killed him and made off with the computer. Perhaps Gricar had uncovered high-level corruption, something so potentially damaging he could only store the evidence on his personal laptop. Maybe he offered the person a chance to come clean, setting up a meeting just outside of Centre County's jurisdiction where he could lay out the gathered information in seclusion. Give them some time to think it over.

Zaccagni points to the park. "He's contemplating what this guy should do, and this guy shows up and this ends up becoming a homicide because Ray doesn't understand how dangerous this man is."

But if it's a clandestine meeting, why spend the day looking at antiques with some woman? Why spend the night there?

Theory two: suicide. The family history supports this. Tony Gricar tracked down aerial photographs of both the site where his father's car was found by a river in Dayton and from North Water Street where Ray's car was parked by the Susquehanna. The similarities are striking. The placement of the bridges, the rivers, and the cars are mirror images of each other.

Zaccagni thinks maybe Gricar kept a diary on his laptop. Maybe that's why it's gone. He was traveling to parks to think it through. "We know [that on Thursday, April 14] he was at another big body of water," says Zaccagni. "He's over in the Huntingdon area. Raystown Dam. We have some people who saw him there." But no one has ever known Gricar to keep a journal. And he was making plans, looking forward to traveling after retirement. Outwardly, he showed no signs of the depression that drowned his brother.

Co-workers certainly noticed no difference in his demeanor. "He did not have any change in his physical appearance or mental state," says Mark Smith, Gricar's first assistant. "The entire office is baffled by his disappearance."

And finally, suicide is a private act. Why invite someone to smoke inside your car before you jump off a bridge?

Theory three: hoax. Gricar was seen with a woman at the antique mall, though witnesses can't say for sure if they were romantic. She could have been a smoker, though Gricar abhorred the habit. Was Lewisburg their rendezvous before skipping town and starting a new life?

Even the computer makes sense. He'd been communicating via e-mail, Zaccagni speculates, playing devil's advocate. "It's all on the laptop. Maybe some directions. Maybe he's been doing some on-line banking, because he has a special account set up in a different name." So he took it with him. And he took the laptop out of the bag to buy some extra time.

The biggest problem with this theory is his daughter, Lara, whom Gricar cared for after a skiing accident in 2001. Lara, whom all his secretaries knew to patch through whenever she called, or face the most severe reprimand. But Lara has not been contacted by her father. She recently took a lie-detector test to prove it.

Further evidence only adds to the confusion.

On July 30, 2005, two fishermen pulled the laptop from the Susquehanna, under a bridge directly behind the park where Gricar was last seen. The hard drive had been removed. And that could not have happened in the fall. In order to remove the hard drive from Gricar's computer, you had to first unscrew it.

On September 23 of that year, a woman walking the low banks of the river came across a piece of electronic equipment one inch by three inches—a hard drive. This was near a railroad bridge a half mile upstream from where the Mini Cooper was parked. The hard drive is the same make and model as Gricar's laptop, but Centre County did not keep tabs on the serial numbers, so Zaccagni can only assume it's the one he's looking for. We'll never know for sure— five months spent in the Susquehanna damaged the hard drive so

Darrel Zaccagni, the police officer who investigated Gricar's disappearance, believes the prosecutor may still be alive.

badly that even the FBI's best forensic crew could not extract the data it once contained.

State Route 192 (Gricar's route) is not the easiest way to get to Lewisburg from Bellefonte—heading down Route 45 shaves about 10 minutes off the hour-long journey. But it is the more scenic road, winding between two mountains, through sparse villages where fields of seed corn outnumber houses 10 to 1. Only four FM radio stations can be picked up clearly, but sometimes lower-frequency stations sneak through the static, like pale faces glimpsed under water. Evangelical doomsayers, mostly.

Nothing. Nothing. Nothing.

And suddenly, there's Lewisburg, home to Bucknell University. The houses here are victorian or colonial and tower over the main thoroughfares. A movie theater with a tall marquee advertises an upcoming documentary festival. The sidewalks are illuminated by glass orbs hanging from wrought-iron stands.

The bridge above the spot where the fishermen found the laptop is about a quarter-mile long. Zaccagni figures Gricar jumped from the south side of the bridge, where the pedestrian walkway is; if you're going in, why cross the street and climb over a concrete wall to do so? But the river flows south, and the laptop was found north of the bridge.

Nor does it seem that the fall could have killed him. It's only about 25 feet to the water.

So what became of Ray Gricar?

There's a strange connection between Ray's last day and a science fiction book.

Not long before he disappeared, Ray told a friend about Melvin Wiley, the police chief of Hinckley Township, in Medina, who vanished without a trace in 1985. No one knows why Ray brought the subject up. Was he worried the same thing was about to happen to him, or did it sound like a swell idea?

In August 2005, a man in Texas who'd seen a TV report on Gricar's disappearance used his camera phone to snap pictures of someone who looked strikingly similar to the missing man in a Chili's restaurant. He was sitting alone. Patty Fornicola believed it was Gricar, but his nephew Tony said it was definitely not. The FBI analyzed the picture, according to Zaccagni, and concluded that if it was Gricar, he'd had minor plastic surgery.

Zaccagni says Fornicola's identification was clouded by optimism. "She's hoping against hope that Ray is still out there," he says. "She'll deal with why he's doing this to her later."

Since then, there have been other sightings, the most promising of which occurred in a Meijer's grocery store in Columbus. When Tony first viewed the store's surveillance footage, he thought it could be his uncle. But upon closer inspection, he noticed that the man on the tape had a distinct way of walking that was not recognizable. He is sure, now, that it was not Ray.

Crime chatroom fans of the homicide theory are quick to suggest a connection between Ray's disappearance and the death of a man named Billy Joe Leathers a few days later. Leathers was a career criminal whom Ray had once prosecuted. But he was out when Ray vanished. As the search for the missing district attorney intensified, Leathers shot himself in the head, committing suicide. But detectives reviewed Leathers's whereabouts for the days surrounding Ray's disappearance and concluded the two never crossed paths.

Then there's the strange connection between Ray's last day and a science fiction book written by a local professor. Bellefonte police detectives have learned that sometime around 1987, Ray was approached by a professor from Penn State who wrote science fiction novels under the pen name Pamela West. She told Ray she was researching the 1969 unsolved murder of Betsy Ruth Aardsma, a beautiful young woman who was stabbed to death inside the campus library. She told Ray she thought she knew who did it, but didn't think she could publish the man's name without getting sued. According to detectives, Ray told her to keep investigating. Eventually, West used the circumstances of the crime in a sci-fi book titled *20/20 Vision*, which was published in 1990. The main character of the story is an aloof detective named Max Crane, who is about to retire. He drives a distinctive car with personalized plates—as did Ray. In the book, the murder occurs on April 15 (the very day Ray disappeared). A vital clue to solving the case is a bit of ash. Police detectives consider it a promising lead.

Ray Gricar's vanishing is a fascinating mystery best considered on porches overlooking the Susquehanna or in cars driving through the void of Route 192. No one may ever come up with a better explanation than what the old man at the antique mall told me: *Sometimes, out here, people just disappear.*

Anyone with information related to this case should contact Detective Matt Rickard at the Bellefonte Police Department, 814-353-2320. You can also contact the family at www.raygricar.com.

CHAPTER 4

Gemini's Last Dance

The Unsolved Murder of Andrea Flenoury

When Detective Bertina King first saw the body in the canal, she thought it was a young girl. The thin, feminine frame was still submerged and mostly obscured. From the shore, King could see only a hand suspended below the muddy water like a beckoning ghost, attached to the faint outline of a tiny female.

The detective figured as soon as the Akron Fire Department arrived and pulled the victim from the water, she could transfer the homicide to detectives who worked juvenile cases. She was wrong.

It was August 7, 2005, a Sunday morning, and though it wasn't yet eight o'clock, there were already looky-loos across the way, milling about behind the laundromat and saloon, leaning out the doors of the apartment complex downstream. This side of the canal, thankfully, was just a big parking lot, now the sole domain of Akron police.

The parking lot serves a section of the Ohio & Erie Canal Towpath Trail on Manchester Road in sleepy Coventry Township, beside the intersection with Carnegie Road. The intersection has claimed many lives recently. A few months earlier, a man hit the bridge guardrail a little after 2 A.M. and flipped his car upside down, into the river. His neck snapped in the crash, and the car went unnoticed for hours. A year before that, two teenage sisters died in an accident just across the street from the parking lot's entrance. A makeshift memorial signed by friends still stands there, surrounded by flowers. The lot is used mostly by towpath joggers or fishermen. And it was a fisher-man who had seen the hand floating under the waves and alerted authorities. Now, the only thing trolling the canal were ducks, and lots of them. It was impossible to not step in the ducks' feces.

Eventually, the firemen pulled the body from the water. It had been wrapped in chains to keep it submerged. They covered the partially clothed body in a white bag so the onlookers could not see the extent of the trauma. Two things were immediately apparent to Detective King. One: this was not a child, but a young woman. Two: she had not been submerged for long; there was no sign of decomposition.

The victim's prints were fed into the Akron database. The wom-an's name was Andrea Flenoury, age 21. Later, the detective would learn that she was better known to others as Gemini.

Before Andrea Flenoury became one of Akron's most popular strippers, she was a Lordstown High School cheerleader. Lordstown is a proud hamlet just outside Warren but far enough removed from the city to be mostly farmland. The town is not large enough for a zip code of its own so it gets lumped in with the city more often than its residents would like. The majority of the townfolk are white. Andrea was not.

Thumbing through the Lordstown High 2002 yearbook, one finds row after row of students of eastern european stock, broken sud-denly by Andrea's portrait. She stands out as much for her graceful-ness as for her milk-chocolate complexion. She seems self-assured as she leans back in a chair, giving the photographer the best view of her perfectly straight teeth. Her cheerleading pictures are there, too. At five foot three, she was one of the shortest girls on the squad.

Although Andrea graduated from Lordstown, she spent a portion of her high school career in Akron, where her mother moved after a divorce. And it was to Akron that Andrea returned shortly after receiving her diploma. Then, she met Jason Conrad.

Ten years older, Conrad already had kids of his own and opted not to work, claim those who know him, in order to avoid paying child support. He was white, with a dark, bushy mane that fell be-low his shoulders. He lived with his mother in an efficiency near

Flenoury's body was wrapped in chains and dumped into the canal here, a few miles from where she was last seen.

Highland Square but spent most of his time at Andrea's place on the other side of Akron.

Andrea lived in a cramped first-floor apartment on Excelsior Street, sharing a bathroom with the other tenants. The house slumps about its sides, as if it gave up the will to stand straight decades ago. Plastic toy cars rest on the stoop. There's a depressed, poverty-stricken feel to the place, betrayed only by two gray satellite dishes attached to the side wall. Not that Andrea seemed to mind the conditions or the locale. She formed friendships with the other housemates, and it was only a short walk to Dave's Supermarket, where she bought jugs of iced tea on summer evenings.

She tried a typical post-grad day job for a while, selling movie tickets at Regal Cinemas. In August 2003, though, she and a coworker were arrested for using a customer's ATM card to steal gift certificates. Those who remember her at Lordstown High blame this behavior on Akron itself. The girl they knew was not a problem child until she'd spent some time there with her mother.

Not long after the bust at Regal Cinemas, Andrea began stripping. It didn't hurt that Lisa's Cabaret was a quarter-mile walk from the

Flenoury was a star cheerleader during her senior year at Lordstown High, a small school just outside of Warren. *(Lordstown High School yearbook)*

apartment. She had also become friends with Amanda Boggs, who lived in the house, too, and stripped at area haunts when she wasn't pushing wings at BW3. Boggs apparently often covered for Andrea. In later police reports related to Andrea, the number she gave to police was the main phone line for BW3 on Exchange Street.

Over the next two years, Andrea danced at practically every club in town, moving from one to another, following the migration of older men seeking flesh. Lisa's Cabaret, Touch of Class, Rumors, Flashdance Cabaret, Exotica. Wherever the action was, so was she.

As Andrea began making serious jack—sometimes $700 a night— her relationship with Conrad took a violent turn.

In January 2004, they got into a fight at Conrad's mother's place. According to the incident report, Andrea claimed Conrad grabbed her by the neck, then threw her to the ground, beating her head against the floor several times. She told police she then grabbed a knife, which Conrad took from her and held to her face.

Conrad said he was breaking up with her, and that she had pulled the knife on him before he pushed her to the ground. They were both arrested and charged with domestic violence.

It was this report Detective King returned to after Andrea's body was pulled from the water, in August 2005. Andrea's claim that Conrad had grabbed her by the neck was intriguing. Andrea had not drowned in the river—she'd been strangled to death first.

Andrea danced at practically every club in town. Wherever the action was, so was she.

She was also six weeks pregnant.

There was no need to invent a reason to bring Jason Conrad in for questioning. He already had a warrant out for his arrest on two grand theft charges. Detective King and her partner, Detective Steven Null, found him at Andrea's apartment. They brought Conrad into the station and began the interrogation.

Conrad said the last time he'd seen Andrea was the night before, around midnight. She had told him she was going to dance at Lisa's Cabaret. He hadn't been worried when he didn't find her home in the morning. She didn't like walking back by herself late at night, so she would occasionally take a ride from a female co-worker, even if it meant crashing at her place.

At first, he seemed concerned about the baby. When they told him that Andrea was dead, the detectives watched him "fall apart," recalls Detective King. He began to cry. And as he came to realize he was the main suspect, he immediately agreed to a series of tests. "Take everything you want right now," said Conrad, according to the detectives. "She was my life. My life is over now."

Conrad passed a polygraph, and his alibi checked out. A DNA test confirmed he was the father of Andrea's baby.

So Detective Null hit the strip clubs and started turning over rocks.

One of the first things he discovered was that Andrea had lied to Conrad. She had not worked at Lisa's Cabaret for at least two months.

A bouncer who knew Andrea well reported he had seen her walking near Arlington and Exchange around 2:45 A.M. The intersection, not far from her apartment, is a hub for hookers and dealers. The bouncer said he pulled over and offered her a ride. She said she was "okay," though, so he drove on. He, too, gave a DNA sample and has been cleared by detectives.

Based on the timeline provided by the bouncer, Detective Null estimated Andrea was in the river no longer than four hours.

Then the case grew cold.

The manager's office at Lisa's Cabaret is an unused section of an old saloon that was walled in when the dance floor was constructed. The cherry wood bar is dull now, unpolished and dusty. A television sits in the corner, propped up by a set of lockers. In front of it sits John (real name changed by request).

John is a thick, solid mass of muscle, which fills out his navy blue jumpsuit, deftly. His head is bald, making him look distinguished in a way only large black men can really pull off. On this February night, he's watching 19 Action News on the small TV. At first, he doesn't want to talk about Andrea. He doesn't want his business associated with that tragedy. But after a moment, he decides if it can help, he'll tell everything he knows. Andrea was special to him, one of the best dancers he's known. Her stage name was Gemini. And since her death, John hasn't allowed anyone else to use that name. "Somebody comes in here—say they've been using the name Gemini for 40 years—they come in here, they're gonna need a new name."

As Gemini, she would dance to "Peaches & Cream," by Monifah. She used to send some of her money to her mother.

John explains that the dancers at Lisa's Cabaret, like all the clubs he knows of, have no set schedule. If a woman wants to dance that night, she can come down and dance. Any time, any day; Lisa's Cabaret is a 24/7 operation. And in the world of Rubber City stripping,

Flenoury lived in a rundown section of Akron, near Arlington, but hoped for a better life for her child.

there is no such thing as a noncompete clause. "We hope they come here," he says. "But they're free to go down to XTC or the Platinum Horse, that's fine. We hope they're comfortable working here."

He describes Andrea almost exactly as her high school guidance counselor at Lordstown High did: energetic, fun, somewhat high-strung. He says Andrea was smarter than most. She modeled herself after Aaliyah, a singer and actress who died in a plane crash in August 2001, at the age of 22.

He remembers Conrad, too. "He tried to come in here when she was working," says John. "But that's something we don't tolerate. We can't have boyfriends hanging out down here."

John is saying something about anchorwoman Sharon Reed's body when two women enter the room. One is nearly naked, breasts exposed through a sheer top; the other, a strawberry-blonde, wears a long-sleeved purple sweatshirt and jeans. They exchange money, and the mostly naked woman walks back into the main room.

The woman in the purple sweatshirt is the house mother this evening; retired from the pole, she manages the small group of strippers and tends to their needs. Heather (name changed at her request)

When she was at work, Flenoury was known as "Gemini." *(Lisa's Cabaret)*

was here before Andrea started and helped show her the ropes. "She always wanted people to laugh," Heather recalls. "If you were ever in a bad mood, she could make you smile. We were like her second family, I think."

Heather became concerned about Andrea's relationship with Conrad long ago. They were always arguing, for one. She never understood what Andrea saw in him, believing he won her over by persistence more than charm. At least Andrea could feel secure that he would always be there for her. "Why he had that pull on her, I can't tell you," she says, shaking her head in frustration.

"When she started, Andrea worked the day shift," says Heather. "That changed about a year ago. When she started working third shift—that's 10 P.M. to 6 A.M.—she started having problems. She wasn't the same person anymore. She wasn't as easygoing. She didn't seem happy. I think she got into some things she couldn't handle."

Heather, however, will not elaborate.

Only in the last few months did Heather notice a change for the better. "She was trying to get her life back on track," she says. "I think the reason she stopped stripping was she found out she was pregnant. The last time I saw her, she looked happy. She was talking about getting a job at McDonald's."

A manager pulls a photograph from the lockers. It's Andrea's last glamour shot, taken just before she quit. Her hair is shorter, her eyes darker, and she's wearing a turquoise bikini top, but she still has that honest smile.

Jeff, the bouncer at Flashdance Cabaret, is a brawny white dude with black hair in a bowl cut and tatts running down both arms. He knew Andrea. Says she was fired because of her tendency to leave with customers.

According to a police report from April 2004, Andrea once left with a patron named Angel Perry, a 19-year-old, freckle-faced kid who appeared harmless enough. When Andrea realized he wasn't driving toward her apartment, she demanded he turn the car around. When he didn't, she began honking the horn to alert the attention of other drivers along Route 8. Perry lost control of the vehicle momentarily, rammed a cement wall, then continued on. She tried to call 911 on her cell, but he snatched it from her and threw it out the window. When he stopped at a red light, Andrea managed to get out of the car and ran to a gas station. Perry was charged with kidnapping. He's not a suspect in Andrea's murder, however, because he was in jail at the time on a parole violation.

Bouncer Jeff also remembers Conrad's temper, from when he temporarily worked at Lisa's Cabaret. "He brought three or four of his buddies in with him," he says, "He would have Andrea give them free dances. I watched him come in angry one night and rip her off the stage."

"If it wasn't him, it was a stalker," says a dancer who's been sitting nearby on an elderly gent's lap in the mostly empty lounge. As she talks, Laura (not her real name) takes off her shirt and puts on the new one the geriatric brought in for her as a present. She smells faintly of lilac.

"All us dancers get a stalker after a while. When Andrea was in here last year, this guy kept calling her, showing up at the bar, buying her drinks. She knew she had a stalker when she was here."

This is a scenario the detectives also feel is likely, based on interviews with other dancers, who have stalkers of their own.

"And I don't buy that talk that she quit stripping," says the bouncer. "That was her meal ticket. She could have hid her pregnancy. I got a girl in here eight months pregnant, you couldn't tell. [Andrea] talked a lot about leaving town. She needed money to do that."

> "All us dancers get a stalker after a while. She knew she had a stalker when she was here."

Flashdance has made the news in relation to another murder lately. Steven Spade, an eagle scout from Mogadore, was brutally beaten, decapitated, dumped in West Virginia, and burned beyond recognition by a group of people that included Lisa Penix. Penix tended bar at Flashdance. Her boyfriend, Shane Rafferty, and his meth-addict friends who helped him kill Spade, were frequent customers.

Detective Null does not believe there is a connection. Akron's efforts to restrict strip bars to certain areas concentrates criminals there, he says. "When you have that element of people, you're going to find them in that part of town."

Across the canal from where Andrea ended up that Saturday night is an old honky-tonk bar called Sam-E's Lounge. It is quite full by 10 A.M. most days. Sam-E's stays open until 2:30 A.M. on Saturdays and would not be completely empty of all patrons and employees until close to 3:30 A.M.

Next door is Carnegie Coin Laundry, which opens automatically every morning at 5 A.M. and is busy every Sunday morning. The hobby fishermen also begin showing up around 5 A.M. during the summer months, and will occasionally stay overnight, angling by lantern.

This shortens the window for dumping Andrea's body significantly. It would appear she ended up in the canal sometime between 3:30 A.M. and 5 A.M. But no one at these businesses, nor in the

The strip club where Flenoury worked was later forced to close for promoting prostitution.

apartments which look out over the dumpsite, recalls seeing anything out of the ordinary until the police arrived the next morning.

The corner of Manchester and Carnegie is a 12-minute drive from where Andrea was last spotted at 2:45 A.M. Arlington will take you most of the way. Still, it would have taken time to bind her in chains somewhere private before transporting her body out of town. And yet, somehow, her killer was not seen. At least not by anyone who is willing to speak to detectives.

Outside of Akron, few know the story of Andrea's tragic end, or how close she was to leaving the nightlife behind. Her story was not told with the same fervor as similar cases involving abducted and murdered white women. No memorial sits at the bank of the canal where she was found.

Her parents are reluctant to speak to the media. In 2006, Andrea's father set up a scholarship in his daughter's name at Lordstown High. It's for cheerleaders who are interested in higher education.

Those hard luck cases who frequent the red light streets of Akron have begun to wonder lately if Andrea's murder was Act 2 of a serial killer's spree. The body of Donna Pittinger was found floating in the

Tuscarawas River in Lawrence Township in April 2005. But, as with Andrea's death, it didn't make prime time news because Donna was also a prostitute with a history of drug addiction. Donna's story only gained attention in late 2007, after armchair detectives blogging on crime sites started to search the web for tales of other dead hookers and happened upon the details of Donna's tragic end.

Donna danced at the some of the same clubs where Andrea worked the pole. She lived within a block of Andrea's apartment and hooked on Arlington, though usually picking a corner further from Exchange. She was known for her bubbly, outgoing personality. Years ago, she had attended Coventry High School, which is in sight of the canal where Andrea's body was found.

Donna was somewhat of a legend in the underbelly of the city. Clients were so fond of her, they often cruised Arlington, hoping to find her on duty. Some still extol her virtues on seedy website message boards devoted to area prostitution. On USASexGuide.info, a man using the name "Me Tigger" writes this chilling epitaph:

> 10+ years ago she should have been a porn star. I have never ever in my life f***ed a woman with as much energy as she had. Pure nympho in my book. She was into making sure my kahunas were thoroughly drained. I used her as an escort to company xmas/ cocktail parties on a couple occasions. Cleaned her up, dressed her up, wined & dined her and she took care of business. Lost touch with her about 6-7 years ago. Then 2 years ago summer I see her on Arlington. What a fall. She was whacked on crack. The little head let her in the car and big head was sorry his buddy did. Never again. Spring of '05 I hear on the radio that she is holding her breath for a long time.

For the moment, detectives do not believe that the two cases are connected, but they are not ruling out the possibility. "We haven't found any names of suspects that overlap Donna and Andrea's cases," says Detective King. "But, because they were both hookers, we did send the files into the FBI."

There should be one more murder included in that file at the FBI.

On October 6, 2007, the body of Sandra Varney was found inside a room at the Noble Motel on Euclid Avenue in Cleveland. Varney was also a prostitute, known around town as "Little Bit." Sandra's last John had a knack for binding and torture. Her killer bound her wrists with wire and suffocated her with a plastic bag.

Detectives Bertina King and Steven Null may yet bring closure to the Flenoury family. Their list of suspects is shrinking. They remain hopeful, hungry for the day they can look the killer in the eyes and know that Akron's red light wanderers are safe again.

Anyone with information concerning Andrea Flenoury's murder can call the detectives at 330-375-2490. To report an anonymous tip, call Crimestoppers at 330-434-COPS.

CHAPTER 5

The Not So Innocent Victim

The Unsolved Murder of Tony Daniels

The drone of the riding lawnmower sputters to a stop as the young Mexican landscaper maneuvers to the edge of the woods behind the parking lot and kills the engine. The mower's bag is full of fresh clippings and must be emptied. Piles of decaying grass lie among the bracken and stagnant pools of water here.

Javier is short, about five foot five. Large, dark eyes emote his feelings better than words—which is good, because he does not speak a lick of English. He carries the bag into the woods between the office complex and I-90, but deeper this time. He doesn't want to dump all the clippings in one place.

Then he sees it, next to a tiny brown pond. It's the color of alabaster, of drywall. And although Javier has only ever seen such a thing in movies, he knows right away what it is.

Calavera.

Quickly, he races to find a supervisor. Out of the woods now, Javier tries to find someone who can interpret for him the dire meaning of one simple word.

Calavera.

Skull.

Detective Lt. Ray Arcuri sits at a picnic table outside the Westlake police station, eating his lunch. At 39, with a smooth, round face and a full head of dark hair, he looks too young to be in charge of a bureau of detectives. But he's respected in town, admired for his near-photographic memory and his passion for the job.

His walkie-talkie suddenly cuts the silence. A landscaper has found some bones off Clemens Road.

Arcuri calls in the animal control officer to check it out, figuring it's a dead dog or some other creature. The animal control officer, however, tells him it's human. There also appears to be a bullet hole in the back of skull. The rest of the skeleton is MIA.

Soon someone finds a femur. Then, a tibia. Seven bones are found, scattered about the property.

"Grab your camera and hustle down to the site," Arcuri says to Detective Patricia Weisbarth as he jogs back into the office. "I'll be there in a second."

The inner sanctum of the detective bureau is nothing more than a wide room with four desks arranged in open cubicles around the center. The carpet is gunmetal gray and still clean. The desks are orderly, but personalized. Arcuri keeps photographs of his family next to his computer. Tacked to the push-pin wall next to Weisbarth's computer is an *ALF* calendar.

Before he heads to his cruiser, Arcuri makes a couple of phone calls. One is to the Cuyahoga County coroner's office, a request for their trace evidence team. The other is to an outfit called NOSES, which provides cadaver dogs, canines trained to sniff out dead bodies. Then he heads out to see the bones for himself.

Javier's mower is still sitting where he left it. Yellow tape stretches across the edge of the parking lot, sealing off the woods from the employees gathering at office windows and from the local reporters already on their way.

As Arcuri gets out of his cruiser, he slips on a pair of rubber gloves. He is led into the woods, toward the thicket where the landscaper found the skull. No one has touched it yet.

Bending to it, Arcuri pulls the skull from the ground. He turns it around in his hands, looking like some actor playing with a prop in a community production of *Hamlet*. Decomposition is com-

Detective Lieutenant Ray Arcuri points to the location where a landscaper found a human skull.

plete; patches of algae cling to its surface, but no tissue. A clean, round hole is found on the back of the skull, near the top. The lower mandible is missing, but Arcuri notes something unique about the top set of teeth. One molar rests at an odd angle and appears to be capped, the bottom portion discolored, gray like cement. He bags it and sends it with a patrolman to the coroner's office on Cleveland's East Side.

The cadaver dogs fail to locate the torso. Arcuri's not surprised; this victim died years ago, from the look of things. Ohio's erratic weather has stripped away everything except bone, including any personal scent the animals might hone in on. So he searches the old-fashioned way: by lining up his officers two arm-lengths apart and marching through the woods.

Soon someone finds a femur. Then, a tibia. Each time a new bone is discovered, it is carefully sealed in a bag and an orange traffic cone is put in its place. Seven bones are found, scattered about the property.

Some local television stations show footage of the search beginning with the six o'clock news cycle. *Human skull found in Westlake!*

Mae Daniels held the key to her son's identity—an x-ray image of his twisted tooth

The city is affluent, and homicides are rare, making this unfolding mystery all the more tantalizing. *Updates at 11!*

At 7:30 P.M., with the sun on the horizon, Arcuri calls off the search for the night. An officer is assigned to stake out the crime scene until morning. Until then, the detective goes home to his wife and a brood of young boys who look just like him.

It's not even 9 A.M. when Arcuri gets his first call the next day. It's a woman, her voice slippery, thick with a Vietnamese accent. She sounds excited.

Her name is Mai Daniels. Arcuri can barely make sense of what she's saying, but he catches enough to understand she believes she knows whose bones they have found. Daniels believes it's her son, missing since September 27, 1997. He was last seen at his stereo store on Lorain Avenue in Cleveland.

No way could it be that easy, Arcuri thinks. It'll be months before we sort out who that skull belongs to.

"Ray, the coroner's on the phone," an assistant tells him.

Arcuri, however, continues talking with Daniels, trying to discern exactly why she seems so convinced they have found her son.

"Ray, *Doctor Balraj* is on the phone."

"Here, take this call," Arcuri says to Detective Jim Janis, a rugged-looking fellow with a wiry goatee.

As Janis speaks to Daniels, Arcuri talks with County Coroner Dr. Elizabeth Balraj, who explains that her trace evidence team will be returning to the woods, along with an anthropologist from Kent State University. Dr. C. Owen Lovejoy works as a part-time consultant for the coroner's office and has a knack for riddling out the age, sex, and race of a victim from recovered bones.

Janis keeps the frantic mother on the phone a while after Arcuri finishes with the coroner. Like Arcuri, Janis figures it's a long shot, but feels this woman deserves to be heard, if only because of the hopelessness she must have endured since her adult son went missing in 1997.

When Janis is done, Arcuri calls the Cleveland Police Department for a copy of the missing-person report on Daniel's son, Phi Huu Mai, a.k.a. Tony Daniels. The report mentions that Tony was mugged a few months before his disappearance. He was pistol-whipped in the face by his attacker and ended up in the hospital. His mother keeps a copy of the x-rays at her residence.

Arcuri calls Daniels back. "Hey," he says, "Do you still have those x-rays?"

A short time later, Arcuri sits in a cruiser, poring over the flimsy black x-rays, while Janis drives toward the crime scene on Clemens Road.

"Hey, Quincy, what do you have there?" asks Janis, sarcastically.

"You know what, Jim? I think it's him," says Arcuri. "I *know* it's him."

Dr. Lovejoy and forensic pathologist Stanley Seligman are already there when the detectives arrive at the Westlake Woods complex. Dr. Lovejoy tells Arcuri he thinks scavenging animals scattered the bones around the woods. The victim, he says, is likely a white male between 18 and 25 years old.

"When you say white male, could it possibly be a man of Asian descent?" asks Arcuri.

"Yes," says the doctor. "Why?"

Arcuri leads Drs. Lovejoy and Seligman into the lobby of the closest office. He hands over the x-rays. Separately, so as to not influence the other's findings, the doctors each look at photographs of Tony's teeth, which were damaged during the mugging. One molar was chipped and capped. They compare it to the upper teeth of the skull. Both say it is a match.

Tony Daniels has been found. Now Arcuri must figure out how he ended up dead in his sleepy little town.

Mai Daniels's apartment on the east side of Cleveland is littered with a hodgepodge of incongruous religious artifacts. A jade-colored sculpture of Buddha stands below an image of the Last Supper painted onto polished driftwood. The air is stale from lack of ventilation. Pictures of a lost son hang on an old refrigerator in the kitchen.

"I kept thinking he was kidnapped, maybe," says Daniels. "That he was in some man's basement, locked up or something."

She had terrible nightmares while Tony was missing. Whenever she saw a news report about an unidentified body found in the Cleveland area, she called the coroner's office and offered to show them Tony's x-rays again. Each time she hoped it was her boy. She hoped she might be able to finally put him to rest. Instinct told her he must be dead.

Tony was born in Nha Trang, Vietnam, in December 1970. Daniels moved with her son to Saigon a short time later so she could take a job with the U.S. embassy. She was assigned to the payroll department and passed out checks to FBI and CIA agents. Tony's biological father, a Philippine, was not involved in his life. The day before South Vietnam fell to the communist North, Daniels left for America with members of the State Department on planes bound for Honolulu. From there, she moved to South Carolina. In 1978, Daniels came to Lorain County with Tony. She met a man and had a daughter named Elise. She found a job with Luxair, manufacturing air conditioners. Both she and her son became American citizens.

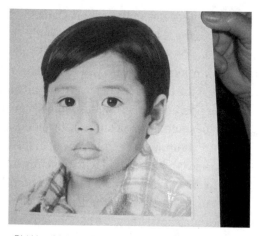

Phi Huu Mai was known as Tony Daniels after he moved with his mother from Vietnam to a rough part of Cleveland.

By all accounts, Tony was a precocious boy. He picked up English quickly, learning to communicate with classmates in Catholic kindergarten. He excelled in studies and was asked to skip a grade. In his spare time, he tinkered with model airplanes. When he was still in grade school, he told his mother he wanted to become a doctor. Those dreams were shattered when he started attending public high school after the family moved to Cleveland.

Daniels says her son was pressured into bad behavior by neighborhood drug lords. He brought home the sort of women that carry around personal drama like some expensive handbag. When he was 17, Tony introduced his mother to a young lady and her baby. He told Daniels that this woman was his girlfriend and that the baby was his.

"I said, 'Tony, that not your baby,'" says Daniels. "It had kinky hair like a black man's and the mother was white."

She figures her son knew the baby was not his but wanted to take care of it anyway. He liked doting on the child, buying clothes and food.

A few years later, Tony enrolled at Ohio State University, where he pursued a business degree. He returned to Cleveland in 1994, to work in the office of Interstate-McBee, where Daniels was employed as a machinist. It was the last legitimate job he had.

Tony found his business experience gave him an advantage over the petty crooks who ran the streets where he lived. His mother didn't know it, but at the time of his death, Tony had his hands in a variety of nefarious operations. He had his mind set on one goal: to become the next king of Cleveland.

Daniels says her son was pressured into bad behavior by neighborhood drug lords.

Propped up against a wall in the Westlake office is a large board with a picture of Tony in the center. Radiating out from his photo, like spokes on a wheel, are other pictures. Most of these are mug shots. They are connected to Tony's photo by a maze of dark marker lines, showing their relationship to the departed. This piece of accidental art keeps the case organized in the minds of the detectives. Almost everyone on that board had motive to kill.

Arcuri points a finger at the picture closest to Tony, a mousy-haired woman with a thin face. She has dark patches under her eyes but is not unattractive.

"This is Tony's girlfriend at the time of his murder, Tara Shores," he explains. "He was living with her in an apartment. They ran an escort company called TNT, which stood for 'Tony and Tara.' Used to advertise in local papers."

The detective points to another woman, this one a platinum blonde, her hair cut short. Her face is fresh, her eyes alluring. "This is Tina Mave. Tony was seeing her, too. She was a prostitute, same as Tara. But Tina was married at the time to this guy, Frank Mave." Frank Mave is a hard-looking type with narrow eyes and a ruddy complexion.

"The night before he disappeared, Tony spent the night at the Lakewood Days Inn with Tina Mave. They checked out around noon on September 27, 1997. Then, Tony rented a U-Haul and spent that day moving equipment into his new business at 10228 Lorain Avenue."

The shop was called T&O Music Express, for "Tony and Omar."

Daniels once aspired to become a doctor.

Omar was a good friend who lived on the East Side, but he had little to do with daily operations. On the surface, it was a used stereo and electronics company. In reality, Tony was using the store to move stolen goods. His stereos were hotter than the streets of Cleveland on a sultry summer afternoon.

"Tony's sister, Elise," Arcuri gestures to a woman with dark hair pulled back in a ponytail, "called his cell phone that afternoon. She wanted to use Tony's credit card to set up a security alarm for her apartment. Tony told her he was on his way to return the U-Haul. He said his friend Sherman was following him in Tony's Bonneville to bring him back home."

Sherman Kyle is a black man with well-trimmed hair and a plastic smile. "Sherman was close to Tara Shores," says Arcuri. "Sherman says he last saw Tony at the shop, around 10 P.M."

The Cleveland investigators who worked Tony's case when he was still missing focused on Frank Mave. It seemed like every hooker and pimp arrested in Cleveland wanted to implicate Frank Mave in Tony's murder, in exchange for a lighter sentence. Many claimed to have heard Frank Mave threaten Tony. Cleveland police suspected he murdered Tony in a fit of jealousy, after discovering that his wife had stayed the night with him in a hotel. But there was no evidence to support this theory, and Frank Mave would admit to nothing more than small-time drug offenses.

Tony's Bonneville was found abandoned on Silvia Drive, around the corner from Sherman Kyle's childhood home. A few viable sets of fingerprints were found on the passenger side of the car. These were fed into AFIS, the law enforcement Automated Fingerprint Identification System, but nothing matched in 1997. After Arcuri inherited the case in 2005, he ran the prints again. This time there was a hit. The prints matched those of Ejike Thomas-Ogbuji, a self-described local hip-hop artist.

In 1997, Tony had aspirations of becoming a record producer and was working with Thomas-Ogbuji on a rap album. When Arcuri caught up with Thomas-Ogbuji, the man acknowledged being in the Bonneville but could not recall if it was before or after Tony's disappearance. He does, however, clearly remember that it was Sherman Kyle driving. Kyle had wanted to show off a new set of speakers he'd installed.

There was one more piece of evidence Arcuri found interesting. After Tony had been missing for a couple of days, his mother convinced the landlord to let her into the stereo shop. There, she found boxes of pizza and wings and two cans of soda sitting on a table. Daniels also discovered a wadded-up paper towel in the trashcan. It was covered in blood.

Recently, that DNA was matched to a profile in CODIS, the FBI's Combined DNA Index System, compiled from DNA samples taken from incarcerated felons. The blood was matched to a person already known to investigators, a man already featured on their board.

On January 20, Westlake detectives returned to Tony's stereo shop, vacant for several years. They sprayed the floor with a chemical agent that causes blood to glow in the dark. The area around the back door lit up like a psychedelic poster. The blood on the floor was Tony's.

•   •   •

"He wanted to be known as Chinese Tony," says Arcuri, revisiting the site where the skull was found. "He wanted to get his hands into everything."

Smarter than his peers, Tony brought a sense of organization to the petty crimes that ruled the West Side neighborhood where he grew up. He used his friends as lieutenants in separate operations to generate cash, theft, prostitution, drugs, and the record label.

> *Tony brought a sense of organization to the petty crimes that ruled the West Side neighborhood*

"No matter what he did, Tony doesn't deserve to have a bullet put in the back of his head," the detective explains. "The innocent victim isn't always so innocent. But what crime did he commit that would be equal to what happened to him? Somebody got away with murder."

In 2006, Arcuri gave a summary report of the case to Cuyahoga County prosecutors for review. Though all the faces remain on the board, there is a lead suspect.

"There are pieces still missing, but the picture is getting clearer. There still could be someone out there who was a witness, a co-conspirator or someone who later learned about the crime." Arcuri hopes for that phone call.

Before heading back to the station, the detective makes one last circle around the Westlake Woods office complex. The rest of Tony's skeleton may lie under this parking lot, never to be reclaimed. Arcuri points to blue ribbons hanging from young saplings a few feet into the thicket, beside a pond. They mark the location of Tony's femurs and tibias. They are reminders that until his killer is found, he rests uneasy here. It's also a reminder to Arcuri that he is not so far removed from the darker crimes of city beats.

Anyone with information related to Tony Daniels's case can reach the Westlake detectives at 440-871-3311.

CHAPTER 6

The Ted Conrad Affair

Cleveland's Strangest Unsolved Bank Heist

It seemed like such a simple story.

On Friday, July 11, 1969, 20-year-old vault teller Ted Conrad walked out of Society National Bank in downtown Cleveland with over $215,000 tucked into a brown paper bag and fled. The FBI and U.S. Marshals Service have been looking for him ever since.

It's one of those unsolved mysteries that every city has in spades, something to be rehashed by local media near the anniversary of the crime, or during sweeps. But newspaper articles I dug up on the subject were mostly superficial retellings, offering little in the way of actual investigation.

When the *Plain Dealer* published a new article about the heist on January 13, I printed it out and set it aside. The article, written by Jim Nichols, was quite good. Nichols found that every time Conrad's classmates from Lakewood High School gathered for a reunion, the FBI was there in case the fugitive stopped by. Nichols printed the name of Conrad's ex-girlfriend—Kathleen Einhouse—but I noticed he hadn't contacted her. I thought that might be a way at fresh information, if I ever got around to writing an article myself.

On Monday, March 24, while cleaning my desk, I found the article again. Underneath it was an e-mail my editor at the newspaper had sent me on January 3. The subject line was: "d.b. cooper." The message was short and contained a link to a website. "This says the fbi has reopened the case," it read.

D.B. Cooper is the name given to the man who hijacked a 727 in 1971 and demanded $200,000 in cash, as well as two parachutes, for the safe return of the passengers and crew. Cooper got what he wanted and somewhere over the state of Washington, he bailed out the back of the plane with the loot. The FBI has been searching for Cooper—whose real name was most certainly *not* Cooper—ever since.

Did the FBI think Ted Conrad was D.B. Cooper?

So, the FBI reopened the D.B. Cooper case about 10 days before a new story on Conrad suddenly appeared in the local daily. I saw the *Plain Dealer* article contained quotes from Scott Wilson, the FBI's Cleveland bureau spokesman. I wondered . . . did the FBI think Conrad was Cooper?

It was enough for a phone call, I figured.

Wilson was on vacation, so I spoke to Special Agent James Keesling, who was filling in. Keesling said he had recently transferred to Cleveland from the Washington office currently handling the Cooper investigation. It seemed like a weird coincidence. I asked him if the FBI thought the two crimes were connected. He said he'd get back to me.

My interest now thoroughly piqued, I searched Whitepages.com for Kathleen Einhouse's phone number. Chances were she'd have married and changed her name since 1969. She probably didn't even live in Lakewood any more. But I tried, anyway. I got lucky. A "K. Einhouse" was listed in Lakewood. The woman who answered the phone was Kathleen's elderly mother.

"Ted sent letters to my daughter after he ran away," she said. "But the FBI took them."

She promised to pass along my cell phone number to her daughter the next time they talked.

While I waited for someone to call me back, I pored through old clippings about Conrad, trying to glean fresh clues. The first item on the crime appeared in the *Cleveland Press* on July 15, 1969. Conrad had played it smart—he stole the money on a Friday, at closing time, giving him a full weekend to escape before a bank manager would notice the shortage on Monday. The FBI weren't alerted until

Ted Conrad's last known photograph, taken at a party before he fled. *(FBI)*

Tuesday, the same day the newspaper printed his school picture. By then, Conrad was long gone.

His method was elegantly simple. July 10, the day before the heist, was Conrad's birthday. On Friday, he made a point to show everyone the bottle of Canadian Club whiskey he'd bought from the store across the street to celebrate his twentieth. He carried it around in a brown paper bag all day. When he left the vault at the end of his shift, no one—not even the security guard—bothered to check his bag. They assumed they knew what was in it. But actually, the bag contained a 10- to 12-inch stack of $100 bills.

Bank managers were stunned to discover the ruse on Monday, after Conrad failed to show up for work. In eight months, Conrad had never missed a day. He had seemed like such a fine young man! "An excellent employee, with excellent credentials," said co-workers. "A lovely boy, a gentleman in every way," said his landlord, who

Theodore J. Conrad

FBI Hunts
$215,000,
Teller Here

Teller Is Missing in Bank Shortage Put at $200,000

A young vault teller at the Society National Bank's Public Square office was being sought by the FBI today in connection with the embezzlement of about $200,000.

CONRAD

FBI agents said Theodore Conrad, 20, of 10600 Clifton Rd., failed to show up for work yesterday. A check by bank officials disclosed a large sum was missing.

Bank officials were conducting an audit to determine the exact amount taken.

Bank officials described Conrad as "an excellent employee, with excellent credentials." They said he had never before missed a day during his eight months with the bank. As a vault teller, Conrad's job was to check money in and out of the vault.

He was described as blond, 6 feet tall, 170 to 190 pounds.

Last Friday he drove off from his apartment, 10600 Clifton Rd., and waved to his landlady, Mrs. Elizabeth Smith, who regarded him as "a lovely boy, a gentleman in every way."

Headlines in the *Plain Dealer* (left) and *Cleveland Press* (right). In 1969, when $2,400 bought you a new Dodge, $215,000 was enough to retire on.

(Cleveland State University Archives)

claimed she saw Conrad get into a cab Friday night and wave to her as the car pulled away.

Also in Conrad's favor was the launch of Apollo 11, on its way to the moon. An entire nation was looking at the sky and could not be distracted long enough to search for a bank robber with a Princeton haircut.

Technically, it couldn't really be called a robbery. Since Conrad worked in the vault, it was considered embezzlement. Whatever you called it, the bank was missing a lot of money. In 1969, when $2,400 bought you a new Dodge, $215,000 was enough to retire on, if invested properly.

A follow-up story ran later that week, tucked in the Metro section, above a piece about Sam Sheppard's new wife passing her citizenship exam. It provided new details about Conrad's personal life. After graduating from Lakewood High School in 1967, with an IQ of 135, Conrad had attended New England College in Henniker, New Hampshire. His father was a professor there. Conrad was voted freshman class president but dropped out and came back to Ohio to be near his mother. She had remarried and lived on Bonnieview Avenue in Lakewood, with his sister, two brothers, and stepfather, Raymond Marsh. Shortly after returning, Conrad got his own apartment on Clifton.

•   •   •

A little after 7 P.M., Kathleen, Conrad's girlfriend at the time of the heist, called my cell phone. I was halfway through a large margarita at El Jalapeños on West 117th Street when she called. If you've never had a large margarita at El Jalapeños, you should know that they are as big as my head and I once won a "largest head" contest (no joke). Luckily, Kathleen 'fessed up to being on her second bottle of wine, so we agreed it was better that I call her back in the morning.

"I have a tape you should see," I vaguely remember her saying.

Head still pounding—why have one large margarita when you can have two for twice the price—I called Kathleen around 11 A.M. She was sitting on a beach in Ocean City, enjoying a short vacation with her friend. Her voice was kind and, it seemed to me, a little mischievous, or playful.

"How did I meet Ted?" she asked, repeating my question. "Geez. Let's see. I was with two friends, driving down Detroit and there Ted was, walking on the sidewalk. I went to St. Augustine, so I didn't know him, but one of my friends did and she said, 'Oh my God, that's Ted Conrad! I heard he just broke up with his girlfriend.' He was very handsome, you know? So we stopped. Anyway, he and I started dating. And we dated until he robbed the bank."

Kathleen paused for a moment, then said, "I have this tape you should see. It's pretty old. VHS. It's a news story about Ted. There's lots of stuff on it." She said she'd make a copy of it and send it to me. She also recommended I watch the original *Thomas Crown Affair*, the one starring Steve McQueen. The summer of '67, Conrad had dragged her to see it twice and had even gone again without her. After each viewing, he would light a cigar and smoke it while he gushed about the film.

I wanted to know about the letters Conrad had sent after skipping town. But she couldn't remember much.

"It was just things about our life together. He said, 'I blew it for $250,000.' And he called me once, too. He said he'd read that thing about his landlady saying he waved to her from the cab. He said, 'I did not wave.' We were all excited when he called. My friends were over and everyone said, 'hello.' He said he'd been in a library and had researched statistics on how often the FBI caught the people they go after. He said, if you get enough head start, 'They're not real good.'"

When she heard that Conrad had stolen the money, she wasn't surprised. He had told her he was going to do it, although she claims she didn't think he was really serious. "He liked to think that he could pull off a heist like Steve McQueen," she said. "He threw it out at a party, once. Told everyone how he was going to do it. He told us he was only going to take money that the bank was storing for some racetrack. He said the money coming in from the racetrack was not counted. The serial numbers weren't logged."

Kathleen may have even, unwittingly, told Conrad how to obtain fake identification. "I had just gotten my social security card and I told him how easy it had been to get a copy of my birth certificate from the bureau of vital statistics. You just went in, looked in a book, pointed to the one you wanted and they gave you a copy. All you needed to get a social security card at the time was a copy of a birth certificate."

The weekend Conrad disappeared, he told Kathleen he was going to see his mother perform in a concert—she was a musician with the Pittsburgh Symphony. He said he was going to stay in Erie. "But then he called me that night. He said, 'Why don't you stop over?' Thank God I didn't."

Kathleen claims that before Conrad took off, he left clues in his apartment that would send the FBI on "a wild goose chase." Things like hair dye and specific references to certain cities he was avoiding. He was going to miss his best friend Rusty's wedding, so he also left behind a piece of paper stuck to his TV set that said, "Rusty, here's your present." Unfortunately, she could not remember Rusty's last name.

Wherever Conrad ended up, he stopped contacting her in the fall of '69—he probably realized the feds were tapping her phone. She figures Conrad went to Canada, because he spoke fluent French. "He wasn't a stupid guy," she said. "He's probably on an island somewhere. I lived on St. Croix for awhile. Have you ever been on

Years later, the FBI constructed the images on the right to show what Conrad might look like as an older man. *(FBI)*

an island? You'd never find someone there. I know some people who have gone to St. Croix on vacation and just stayed. It's so un-regulated."

There was one other thing Kathleen mentioned in that first con-versation. A book had been written about Conrad in the '70s—*Move Over, Steve McQueen*. A friend of hers happened upon it at a garage sale. "It's completely, totally inaccurate," she said. "At least the stuff about the girlfriend." I found two copies of the book for sale on the Internet. One was listed at over $300. The other, available on eBay, was marked at $29.95—shipping included. The eBay listing also had a picture of the front page. It was signed by the author—Jeff Keith. It read, "To Josephine, to our West Virginia agent, with best wishes, Jeff."

I added it to my shopping cart.

Special Agent Keesling called me back early in the afternoon. He had checked with his old co-workers in Washington state—Conrad was not considered a suspect in the D.B. Cooper case. The timing of the *Plain Dealer* article had been coincidence.

Darn.

•   •   •

The next day I called Kathleen again. She had been thinking about Ted and remembered more details about her long-lost love. "We used to have this ritual on Friday nights. There was a seafood place next door to his apartment and they got fresh shrimp on Fridays so he would buy some shrimp and a bottle of champagne and we'd go back to his place."

"And the FBI almost got him in Hawaii, in 1969, I think," she continued. "A couple from Ohio were on vacation and spotted him at a bar. I think the FBI found a pewter mug there that I had given Ted as a present. I think that's how they know it was him, for sure. It had his initials on it."

Since we had talked, Kathleen had found an old letter, written to her by a friend of Conrad's named Mike Murphy, who was visited by the FBI while stationed in Germany in 1969. She read the letter into the phone. "'If you happen to be thinking at this moment that they wanted to ask about Ted, you are correct. They took me outside, asked me a number of pertinent questions like, when did I last hear from him, did he ever mention anything about this to you? I finally got back inside to a cold pizza and warm beer.'"

After giving it some more thought, she really felt that Conrad must have gotten a new identity worked out before leaving Lakewood and had probably found a name to use at the vital statistics office.

Having recently written a story about a man in Eastlake who stole someone's identity in 1978 (Chapter 10: Hiding in Plain Sight: The Unsolved Suicide of Joseph Newton Chandler), I knew one way such a thing could be done. "Sometimes, people who need to hide will use the name of someone they knew, someone who would have been about their age, but died in a tragic accident before they were old enough to collect a social security card," I said. "Was there anyone you and Ted knew who was about your age, who died?"

"Actually, yes," she said.

A friend of Kathleen's had a younger brother who died in an accident in Lakewood. The boy's name had been Tim Greenrod.

An online directory search found no Tim Greenrod in the United

States. If Conrad was using the name, he wasn't in the phone book.

I contacted a friend of mine named Mike Lewis, who runs Confidential Investigative Services, a local private-eye firm. He ran the information through a system that compiles names, phone numbers, and addresses pulled from public records, credit reports, and magazine subscription lists. He got a hit.

Lewis sent me an e-mail with the results of his search for Tim Greenrod. Someone using that name, with a birth date that matched the deceased, was associated with an address right here in Cleveland.

> *Every time Conrad's classmates from Lakewood High School gathered for a reunion, the FBI was there.*

Later that afternoon, I pulled into the driveway on Linn Avenue listed in Lewis's report. It was a bad neighborhood, a section of rundown houses off Broadway. Metal bars obscured windows that looked out over the smokestacks of Mittal Steel. Ugly dogs barked incessantly at strangers, held back by wire and thick chain link fences.

The house, which someone using a dead boy's name had once listed on some form, was vacant and neighbors said that no one had lived there for a long time. The house has a mailbox hidden from the road, though, and I wondered if it was possible someone used this abandoned property as a safe place to pick up mail. I looked around. The mailbox could be seen by two homes.

At the house closest to the mailbox, a young woman answered the door, flanked by a small child.

"Do you know anyone who uses that house?" I asked.

"Victor," she said.

"Is Victor white?"

"Nah. Only white guy around here lives there," she said, pointing to the other house that could see the mailbox. "He's kind of an older man."

But that house was vacant, too. The windows were smashed and there was no car in the driveway.

Jeff Keith wrote a "fictional-ized" account of Conrad's crime. Some think it might not be fiction at all.

I left a message for Victor, but he never called.

Waiting in my mailbox when I returned home was my copy of *Move Over, Steve McQueen*. I scanned the author's bio—"Jeff Keith," it read, "was born in Cleveland, Ohio, in 1949 . . . by the age of 10 he spoke French fluently." I set the book aside for the moment. That evening, I watched The *Thomas Crown Affair*, taking notes, because Kathleen was quite convinced that Conrad had studied the film and McQueen's performance.

Whereas the newer version of the movie—the one starring Pierce Brosnan—has Crown stealing priceless art, this classic was a well-staged bank heist. Crown hired patsies to rob the bank for him. And the first thing he did after the heist was light up a stogie. After depositing the $2.6 million in a Swiss bank account, Crown returned to the states and fell for the woman hired by the insurance company to catch him. He offered her a chance to go with him, but in the end left her behind.

Thomas Crown, Ted Conrad. T.C., T.C. It was hard to tell where one began and the other ended.

The next day, Kathleen's package arrived via overnight express. Inside was a DVD copy of the VHS news report she'd kept for 20 years, a 1986 segment by Bill McCay that had aired on a local station. It was about 20 minutes long and gave a few details that I had not found in newspaper articles.

Most interesting were a few snippets from the actual letters Conrad had mailed to Kathleen in the days following the heist. "I do want to write, though I only ask that you burn my envelopes so the authorities don't get the postmarks!"

But the FBI intercepted the letters. One was dated July 15 and had been deposited at the Washington D.C. airport. A second letter was dated July 17 and postmarked "Inglewood, CA."

An FBI agent revealed that Conrad had been making audio recordings of his phone calls to Kathleen. The tapes are played in the report.

"Have you played your Beach Boys album, yet?" Ted asks in his too-innocent voice.

It's impossible to make out her response.

"Very good," he says. "That's what counts. Everybody else make it home okay? Oh, I'm keeping you from your friends!"

"It's okay," she says. "It's my turn."

Conrad, according to McCay's report, is left-handed, enjoys golfing, and is an accomplished billiard player.

The report confirmed Kathleen's story about the couple in Hawaii. They were from Beachwood, and claimed to have met Conrad in the Princess Kauai Hotel bar.

Apparently, Conrad wasn't as smart as he thought he was. Further letters reference the statute of limitations for embezzlement—seven years. Unfortunately for Conrad, the statute of limitations became meaningless when the federal government indicted him in December of 1969.

"Maybe on that 7th year, we'll meet and fall in love," he wrote. "It's now seven days and only six years, 358 days to go!"

The report ended with a statement from Conrad's father. "This is the heartbreaker of my life," he said.

·　　·　　·

Move Over, Steve McQueen was a fast read: 133 well written pages, crafted in a style undoubtedly inspired by Hemingway, Salinger, and, at the end, Faulkner. It claims to be a novel.

The main character is Ted Conrad. Worried about the draft, he enrolls at Cuyahoga Community College to avoid going to war. He gets a job at Aero Kit, Inc., a Rocky River factory that produces rubber gaskets for the war machine. There, Conrad befriends an assortment of colorful characters and sort of falls for an older married woman. Eventually, he gets an interview at Society National Bank, and the president is so taken by him that Conrad is made "vault teller."

In various places throughout the book, the writer drops French idioms or lapses into the language during conversations between Conrad and his mother. The girlfriend, Cheryl Ann Miller, bears little likeness to Kathleen.

On page 89, during a conversation between Conrad and his friend "Russell Dunn," Russell warns his friend that his clever plan might not work. "Don't you think someone's gonna *see* a paper bag and check it?"

"That's just it!" says Conrad "I'm depending on *everyone* looking but no one seeing!"

Finished, I closed the book and set it face down. On the back was the author's photo. For a moment, it felt like I couldn't breathe.

I ran "Jeff Keith" through a newspaper archive search. This headline came up: "How One Lawyer Tormented His Victims and the Justice System."

"People will tell you Jeffrey Keith is the devil himself, but officially, he is inmate No. 182622 in 7 Delta Pod of the Cuyahoga County Jail," it began.

In 1995, Keith had been convicted of a litany of arson charges and sentenced to 25 to 50 years in prison. The prosecution proved that Keith had terrorized his ex-girlfriend by hiring a man to torch the cars and homes of just about anyone she knew.

The article described Keith as a lawyer from Lakewood who didn't practice law and who ran unsuccessfully for City Council four times, a clever, maniacal sociopath who owned three properties and kept different women at each. One woman claimed Keith had locked her and her children in the house on weekends while he drove to Erie, Pennsylvania, to visit his other girlfriend. She said that when Keith found out she was pregnant—with his daughter—he talked her into an abortion because he only wanted a son.

He was also a member of a local middle eastern organization, to which he donated $30,000, but got kicked out after he started dating the president's daughter. At about the same time, 46-year-old Keith started dating a high school senior he met on a levy campaign, in Parma.

When he was indicted on the arson charges, that high school senior told the police some odd things about Keith. She said Keith had a lot of money but never worked. She claimed he had a safe-deposit box in which he kept gold teeth and coins, according to the article.

He was also in trouble for forging an old lady's will.

Assistant county prosecutor Steven Dever sent Keith away for a long, long time. And Keith was not happy.

In 1996, Keith was indicted again—this time for plotting to kill a firefighter and the prosecutor who put him away. But those charges didn't stick. A woman named Barbara Loesser, who worked as a reporter for the failed alternative weekly *Downtown Tab*, contacted the prosecution's witnesses—using the name Chris Lawrence—and intimidated them until they recanted or changed their stories. Prosecutors noted that *Downtown Tab* was owned by James Carney Jr., a friend and associate of Keith's, although Carney was never charged. Loesser was indicted for bribery, intimidation, obstructing justice, and perjury. She, too, is now on the run and wanted by police.

I had one more call to make that night. On the envelope in which the book was sent, the return address listed a "Josephine Mackin" and a West Virginia address. I assumed it was the same "Josephine" that had once been Keith's agent. Maybe she could provide some information about whether there was ever a partnership between Keith and Conrad.

Apparently, however, "Josephine" is a popular name in West Virginia. The woman was not the same Josephine who had once been Keith's agent. She claimed to have found the book at an estate sale four years ago.

Mondays at the paper are busy as everyone rushes to make deadlines. But I needed to share a wild theory with my editor.

"Do you have five minutes to hear a story?" I asked my editor, Frank, peeking into his office.

"Sure," he said.

I sat down and placed a newspaper clipping that showed Ted Conrad's school photo on his desk. Quickly, I gave a brief synopsis of Conrad's crime. Then I set *Move Over Steve McQueen* next to the article, face up. I told Frank about the strange insight the author had into Conrad's actions and motivations, how it pretended to be fiction, how the author was fluent in French, was born the same year as Conrad, and seemed to have a lot of money but reportedly did little work. Then I flipped the book over. The photo on the back was taken in 1977, and the guy had a handlebar mustache and longer hair, but...

"I think it's the same guy," I said.

"I see a resemblance," said Frank.

"The chin and the ears are the same," I said.

"Look at the left eyebrow," said Frank. "It dips in here and here, just like Ted Conrad's."

The art director concurred. "I'd buy it," he said.

I called the Trumbull Correction Institution where Keith is being held while he awaits his first parole hearing in 2018. I could submit a request to meet with Keith, but it was up to him whether or not he would see me. I faxed a letter explaining that I had a copy of his book and wanted to talk to him about his inspiration for writing it.

While I waited for an answer, I tried to find some kind of verification that Keith was who he claimed to be.

.　　　.　　　.

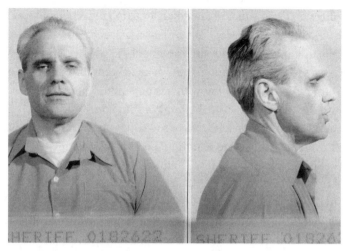

In 1997, Jeff Keith was sentenced to serve 20 years and 6 months in federal prison at the Trumbull Correctional Institution. He says he's not Ted Conrad. *(Cuyahoga County Sheriff's Office)*

There is an office at City Hall where the names of everyone born and everyone who has died in Cleveland are kept in large black binders, arranged by year. It's a weird, off-putting place. It feels a little like some modern-day re-invention of Greek mythology.

I was looking for proof that the real Jeff Keith had died and Ted Conrad had stolen his identity, like someone had apparently stolen Tim Greenrod's.

I quickly located the birth certificate for a "Jeff Keith" in 1949, the only "Jeff Keith" listed that year. I combed the dead files for the years immediately after 1949, hoping to find "Jeff Keith" again. I didn't. However, I did find a "Baby Boy Keith" who died in 1950, shortly after childbirth. That child's father had the same name as the father listed on Jeff Keith's certificate. But the mother's name was different.

Later that day, a spokesperson with the prison called to say that a conference room had been reserved for tomorrow—Keith had agreed to meet me.

On the way home, I dialed a number I had found for the real Jeff Keith's mother, based on information taken from his birth certificate. An aged woman's voice answered. "Hello?" I explained, as best

I could, who I was and that I needed her to tell me if her son was the man who had written *Move Over, Steve McQueen*.

"No, that man is not my son," she said.

It was the answer I wanted, but I sensed something in her voice. "Ma'am, I'm real sorry. I know this is personal. But I really need to know if the man who wrote the book is your son."

There was a long pause. "He's my son," she said. "He is. But I don't want anything to do with him. I'd like to forget it."

I called Frank and told him, "Jeff Keith is not Ted Conrad."

"Are you *sure*?"

"In order for it to work, he would have had to steal not only his name, but his mother's and sister's, too. Yeah, I'm sure."

"So how did he know so much about Ted?" asked Frank.

Good question.

"I knew Ted from Aero Kit," said Keith, the next day. We sat in a tiny room, with a prison official monitoring our conversation quietly from the corner. Keith is a handsome man, with a high forehead below his smartly-combed white hair. He made eye contact and spoke eloquently, slipping into French occasionally. "I was Ted's boss at the factory, even though I was only 18. We worked the night shift. Some people walk into a room and it lights up. Ted was that kind of guy. He was not arrogant in any way."

On the table in front of us was a folder that Keith had put together. It was full of material about the history of the '60s, in order to give some perspective on the time period when the heist occurred.

"Look, the first and last Catholic was elected President, we were at war, and we had The Pill," he explained. "We created recreational sex. All these things threatened to tear apart the fabric of the country. In the middle of this mirage, Ted Conrad watches a movie called The *Thomas Crown Affair* and he gets an idea about how to escape it all. It's hard to find one man fleeing when everyone is running from something, right?"

So what happened to Conrad?

"Ted went to Canada," said Keith. "Toronto. He posed as a draft dodger on Yonge Street."

"How do you know that?" I asked.

"I know, okay? I know," he said. "In 1969, there were 10,000 draft dodgers going through Toronto. If you explained that your father was in the military—Ted's dad was a Navy man— then they set you up with a fake ID. After that, Ted went to Montreal. He had a French nose. You know what that is? It means when you speak French you sound like a Frenchman. He disappeared for good, there. Maybe even he went to college, got a degree, somewhere like McGill University."

> "Kid kept telling me to let him go. That he was some Robin Hood. He was nothing more than a thief."

"How do I find him?" I asked.

"You won't find Ted. He'll find you. Make enough noise, he'll find you. Maybe through e-mail."

"Where was he the last time you spoke to him?" I asked.

Keith looked at the prison official, then back to me, with a smile. "That's a sneaky question," he said. "I'd say Montreal is where he evaporated. That I'm pretty sure of."

Before I left, I asked Keith why he had written "our agent" when he signed the book for Josephine. He shook his head. "I can't remember," he said.

Retired Deputy U.S. Marshal Pete Elliott pursued Conrad for nearly 40 years. His son now runs the office in Cleveland.

"I was interested in the case, because Conrad lived in my neighborhood," Elliott said. "I knew kids who knew him. They kept telling me to let him go. That he was some Robin Hood. I told them that he was nothing more than a thief."

In 1969, it wasn't yet standard procedure for bank employees to be fingerprinted. So Elliott methodically back-tracked paperwork that Conrad had signed at the bank, papers that he had to have touched. From those sheets of paper, crime lab technicians were able to isolate several latent prints, but not a complete set. Still, it was enough to compare to suspects as they popped up, which is exactly what they did in the mid-1980s, when a man who matched Conrad's description was arrested in Honolulu. Elliott flew out to Medford, Oregon, where the man was being held, but the fingerprints did not match.

Elliott has always suspected Conrad may have fled to Canada.

"What would I say if I saw him tomorrow?" Elliott laughs. "I think I'd just like to say, 'Gotcha!'"

Before he hangs up, Elliott leaves me with the real name of Ted's good friend—Russell Metcalf. I find a man with that name still living in Ohio, but the number is unpublished, and there isn't enough time to drive out to his house before the story's due.

On a whim, I enter a few searches into Google before sitting down to write about my short but strange search for the elusive Ted Conrad.

"Ted Conrad Montreal."

Nothing.

"Bank Heist Montreal."

Nothing that speaks to Conrad's flair for the dramatic.

"Montreal *Thomas Crown Affair.*"

Now here's something.

In 1972, thieves climbed through the skylight at the Montreal Museum of Fine Art and made off with artifacts worth over $1 million, including Rembrandt's *Landscape with Cottages*. It was a well-orchestrated and clever caper, listed as one of the "top 10 heists of all time" by Canada's History TV. More than one person has noted the similarities the crime has to the second *Thomas Crown Affair*.

I wonder . . .

CHAPTER 7

Third Time's a Charm

The Unsolved Murder of Ramona Krotine

Jeffrey Krotine is halfway through his hamburger when he notices the manager of the Edgewater Yacht Club walking through the dining room. Krotine's wave catches the man's eye; he stutter-steps to a momentary stop and waves back in awkward recognition. Then he disappears through a doorway and Krotine turns back to his sandwich with a shrug. He's used to this by now.

Ten minutes later, Krotine steps out of the arctic chill of the dining room and into the withering August heat. He wants to show off the sailboat he hopes to buy. His wide hips concealed beneath a casual, bright button-down, Krotine meanders toward a line of boats parked on rollers near the security stand. His hair has mostly given way to gray but has yet to recede. It's cut neatly, a holdover from his time in the army, when he transported Agent Orange in Danang. His smile reveals misshapen, yellow teeth.

"This is the Corvette of sailboats," he says, leaning against a small, sleek Highlander covered in a green tarp, its mast tilted over its hull. "I was going to buy it. But when other members here found out about it, they undercut me." Conspiracy, for Krotine, has become a central theme.

Krotine's sunken eyes look tired and unfocused, half-hidden in wrinkles. It's not age. It's the *mileage*. He stood trial three times for the grisly 2003 murder of his wife, Ramona, enduring two hung juries before a third found him not guilty in May 2005. If he was stalwart in his defense, now he is mostly just numb. The ruling gave him his life back, although it scarcely resembles the one he once had.

Prior to Ramona's death, Krotine earned $325,000 a year, managing a State Farm Insurance office he had cultivated from zilch. A consummate schmoozer, he boasts that he once claimed more auto policies than any other agency in Ohio. When he went out to eat, restaurant owners would stop at his table and chat, not retreat into kitchens.

He and Ramona raised three children in a comfortably modest four-bedroom colonial in Parma, and all of them were heading down the right path. Jeff Jr. was a chemist and was starting a family of his own. Jennifer was studying accounting at the University of Cincinnati. Following in his father's footsteps, youngest son Jason had joined the Marines.

Since then, Krotine has surrendered the family home in Parma. He sold it to help cover his legal bills. His savings, once fattened in the promise of a leisurely retirement, has been drained to keep him fed and clothed. When I caught up with him in 2005, Krotine was living in the stale air of his former office on Rocky River Drive. Worn clothes and dirty dishes cluttered the rooms.

His children maintained their father's innocence at trial, but they don't visit any more. His in-laws, also estranged, are still convinced that he killed Ramona.

There's nothing casual about the way Krotine talks nowadays. His eyes seek out insincerity like well-calibrated robotic sensors. If he's interrupted, he casts his eyes down and raises a protective hand, as if defending against an onslaught of hostile words. He's heard enough arguments for a lifetime; now, the only conversations worth having are those he leads.

Krotine is still navigating his freedom, trying to stitch a life—a personality—together. The boat in the parking lot is one more step toward feeling normal again, toward softening the numbness that enshrouds him.

He gives the boat a gentle pat, then leads the way to a wooden gazebo by the water. A barely perceptible breeze drags across the

Ramona and Jeff Krotine during happier times.
(Jeff Krotine)

waves and plays at his hair. His smile slips away. A pause drifts outward over Lake Erie.

Then Krotine returns to talk of Ramona.

As the sun set on Friday, March 21, 2003, Greg Wilczewski drove aimlessly through Brook Park in search of his missing sister. An employee at the Ryba Fudge booth inside the I-X Center, Ramona had attended an exhibitors' party on Thursday night at the Clarion Hotel in Middleburg Heights. She had last been seen walking to her Toyota Camry around 2:30 Friday morning.

Around 11 P.M. Wilczewski found Ramona's Camry in the parking lot of the Brookpark Road rapid transit station. The car was locked. There was blood on the ground next to the back door. He peered inside and saw more blood on the back seat. Then he shattered the driver's side window with a tire iron and popped the trunk. Inside was his sister's body.

Ramona's face was horribly bruised, the result of blows that split her scalp open in several places. A gunshot wound from close range had left a dark hole above her left ear. Her black shirt was pulled

The Krotine family home in Brook Park. Police believed Ramona was murdered here. *(Cuyahoga County Coroner's Office)*

halfway out of her jeans; her legs were bent behind her, arranged to fit inside the makeshift tomb.

A baby seat had been taken from the vehicle, along with $4,000 Ramona was planning to deposit for her employer that morning. Initially, it appeared to police that she had been the victim of a robbery that had escalated to murder.

By midnight, Brook Park police arrived at Krotine's house to deliver the grim news. Krotine never asked how she died, they later told prosecutors. He appeared to cry, but shed no tears. The police also reported that Krotine had never searched for her. He had gone to work as usual that day, met with a client at noon. He listened to radio news coverage of the U.S. invasion of Iraq, where their son's Marine unit had been deployed. He made numerous calls to Jeff Jr., who had left work to wait at his parents' home, in case his mother returned. Sometime that afternoon, Krotine surfed the Internet for new mattress covers.

For three weeks, police tried to flush out a suspect from sparse leads gathered from people who had been at the party. An autopsy yielded few clues. Then, when detectives drove past the Krotine home one afternoon, they found old carpet on the tree lawn and a work truck parked in the driveway. Krotine was remodeling his bedroom. The walls were freshly painted and the house had been professionally cleaned. Krotine said the new room would honor his wife's memory. It was painted bright yellow, with sun-like crescents on two walls. He told them that in his letters from Vietnam, he had referred to Ramona as his "sunshine."

That night, detectives pulled the carpeting from a trash bin. On it, they found Ramona's blood. Jeffrey Krotine was now the main suspect. The crime scene, they asserted, had been staged.

Detectives spent 10 months methodically building a case against Krotine. On February 2, 2004, he turned himself in and was charged with murder and tampering with evidence. Prosecutors alleged the following chain of events:

Ramona returned from the party late that night and climbed into bed. That's when Jeffrey suddenly turned violent. He beat her skull re-

> *It appeared to police that she had been the victim of a robbery that had escalated to murder.*

peatedly on the wooden headboard, rendering her unconscious. Then he wrapped her body in sheets and carried her to the garage. He removed the baby seat that was in the Camry for a nephew and placed Ramona in the back seat. Jeffrey then drew a 9mm handgun and shot his wife once in the head. He tossed items from her purse onto the floor of the car, perhaps to simulate a robbery, then transferred her body to the trunk and drove into town, where he abandoned the car at the RTA lot.

Cuyahoga County Prosecutor William Mason presented the case to the media with his signature self-assured vigor. He called it an instance of domestic violence that had quickly escalated to cold-blooded murder. By the time the trial began five months later, Court TV had descended upon Cleveland.

The evidence against Krotine was circumstantial, but it was also voluminous.

Ramona's blood was on their bedroom door, on a step leading into the garage, and on the rim of a sink inside their home. A 9 mm handgun Krotine kept in his office was the same basic type that had fired the lethal bullet.

Ramona was seen wearing black heels at the party, but her body was found in bloody socks and spotless white shoes—a mistake made by Krotine in the heat of the moment, Assistant Prosecutor David Zimmerman asserted.

If the killer had simply been a random thief, he wasn't a very good one. Ramona's credit card, checkbook, and wedding ring were not taken, but her key chain was. "The only person who would take those keys would be someone who needs those keys to get back inside his house," says Zimmerman.

> **Most damning, according to prosecutors, was Krotine's behavior in the hours after his wife disappeared.**

Prosecutors also pointed out peculiarities in Krotine's bedroom renovation. The carpet he discarded three weeks after Ramona's death was missing a four-by-six-foot strip between the bed and the bathroom. Krotine, prosecutors claimed, knew that piece would implicate him, so he took extra care in its disposal. After new carpeting was installed, Krotine pulled it up and painted the section of wooden floor once covered by the missing carpet.

"His paranoia got the better of him," says Assistant Prosecutor Anna Faraglia, who tried the case with Zimmerman.

Krotine's explanation for painting the bedroom in his wife's honor was also bunk, they claimed. "Ramona hated the color yellow," says Zimmerman. "The family members told us she hated that color."

Then there was the mistress.

Interviews with former employees of Krotine revealed he had carried on an affair with Mary Engel, a State Farm representative who worked in his office. For two years, they had been having sex in a third-floor room of the office, which prosecutors referred to as their "love nest." Ramona, the couple believed, never knew.

Most damning, according to Zimmerman, was Krotine's behavior in the first hours after his wife disappeared: how he went to work, although he knew that Ramona hadn't come home; how he surfed the web for a new mattress cover; how he reacted in front of police to the news of her murder. Krotine admitted each of these claims.

Yet he also had answers for just about every question. He pulled

After his wife's murder, Krotine redecorated their bedroom and painted part of one wall. He pulled up carpeting and painted a small section of the floor, to cover a stain where he had spilled cognac, he said. *(Cuyahoga County Coroner's Office)*

up the carpeting after he spilled cognac in a drunken stupor, he said. And the carpeting recovered by detectives did not appear to have been vigorously cleaned, as one would expect from a covered-up crime scene. Ramona's blood around the house? Only three drops were on the carpet. The trace amounts found elsewhere could have been left anytime in the past. Moreover, if Ramona had been beaten in the bedroom, the place would have been covered in blood, according to testimony from Cuyahoga County Deputy Coroner Stanley Seligman.

Ballistics tests could not confirm whether Krotine's gun was an exact match to the weapon that killed Ramona. Further, the defense argued, many of Krotine's employees knew that he kept the gun at work—hidden under a hat—not at home. He made no effort to conceal it after Ramona's death.

The Krotines' daughter, Jennifer, had slept in their house the night Ramona disappeared, in a bed just 11 feet from the master bedroom. If a violent struggle had taken place there, how did Jennifer sleep right through it? "She never heard screams, an argument, a beating, a shot—nothing," attorney William Doyle argued.

As for the affair, Krotine admitted to it, and he told his children about it before the trial began.

Police bungling, the defense argued, prevented them from finding the real murderer. Blood from someone other than Ramona had been found under one of the Camry's door handles but Brook Park detectives never attempted to match it to anyone. A red fiber found on Ramona's body was lost, as were leaves that had been found stuck to her back. The defense team fixated on the shoddy work of Brook Park detectives for the better part of three hours before jurors began deliberations. It paid off. On August 4, 2004, the jury announced it was deadlocked at nine to three in favor of conviction. Judge Timothy McGinty declared a mistrial.

Krotine hired four new lawyers for his autumn retrial because his first team told him he no longer could afford them, he says. The prosecution returned the team of Zimmerman and Faraglia, with virtually no changes in their presentation. After three weeks of testimony, 10 of the 12 jurors sided against Krotine. But the two holdouts could not be pressured into changing their minds. On November 30, McGinty declared a second mistrial.

Then Mason called in the big guns. Assistant Prosecutor Steve Dever replaced Zimmerman and reconfigured the approach to the third trial. Dever's predecessors had laid out the circumstantial evidence only superficially, choosing instead to focus on Krotine's odd behavior in the wake of Ramona's disappearance. Actions could be explained away, thought Dever. Science could not.

When the third trial began on April 27, Dever zeroed in on the blood found on the bedroom door and the step inside the garage. Forensic pathologists were called in to testify in detail about the blood evidence.

"Small means a lot," says Dever, referring to the minute drops that were recovered. "It's spatter. When the droplets are that small, it means it's coming at high velocity." According to pathologists, such droplets are the product of a severe beating that happened nearby, not of a typical household cut.

Krotine's defense countered with a surprise of its own. Mel Twining, an I-X Center vendor who saw Ramona at the hotel party, testi-

The killer shot Ramona while she was lying in the back of the car. A baby seat was taken out to make room for her body. It has never been found. *(Cuyahoga County Coroner's Office)*

fied he had stepped outside to smoke that night around 2:30 A.M. He noticed a man standing by a Toyota Camry while someone else struggled to set something in the back seat.

"Later, I thought maybe it could have been someone holding someone down in the back seat," Twining says.

On the stand, Twining stunned jurors with another revelation. The day after the party, he attended a cookout at the house of Susan Ziegler, an acquaintance of Ramona's from the I-X Center. While Twining was there, Ziegler had checked her voice mail; among the messages was one left at 6:45 A.M. that day—a female voice pleading "Help me" in a whisper, before the line went dead.

"It sounded like somebody dying," Twining recalls. Ziegler had testified at the first two trials as well, but neglected to mention the phone call until she was asked about it in the third trial.

Twining says that prosecutors were aware of him for over a year, but that they had greeted his story with anger and told him that he

Ramona's body was found in the trunk of her car at a rapid transit station on Brookpark Road. The white shoe was a crucial piece of circumstantial evidence for prosecutors. *(Cuyahoga County Coroner's Office)*

could hurt their case. "If they treat all their witnesses like me, it's no wonder no one testifies," he says. "I went down there to do some good and got treated terrible."

Krotine believes the prosecution hid Twining, as well as the phone call to Ziegler's house, during the first two trials for fear that such evidence would diminish the case against him.

"That is absolutely incorrect," counters Zimmerman, who says he gave Twining's name to the defense before the first trial.

Some say that the turning point in the third trial came when the Krotines' youngest son, Jason, took the stand. When he spoke of sleeping inside a hole half-filled with water during his stint in southern Iraq, his father broke down and cried. Then came the crucial question.

"If, for one minute, you thought your father brutalized your mother in that house, what would you do?" attorney Richard Drucker asked in a booming voice.

Jason stared calmly back. "He wouldn't be here right now."

On May 27, 2005, Krotine was acquitted.

•   •   •

It's early June, 2005, and Jeffrey Krotine is sharing a booth near the back of the 100th Bomb Group restaurant on Brookpark Road with Mary Engel, the woman with whom he conducted a two-year affair. Engel e-mailed me during the third trial, after the *Plain Dealer* published some of her testimony. She was upset that the paper had laid bare her third-floor trysts with Krotine but hadn't bothered spell her name correctly.

Slight of build, with a high voice and soulful eyes half-concealed under dark bangs, Engel edges in comments occasionally, but Krotine, who took over this conversation early on, shows no sign of letting up. She seems not to mind.

"During the trial, it felt like I was in slow motion and everything around me was sped up," Krotine says between forkfuls of tuna. "After the trial, I feel like I'm in fast-forward and everyone else is in slow motion. I imagine it's kind of like decompression. It's a feeling of coming back into society."

Toward the end of the third trial, prosecutors had offered to reduce the murder charge to manslaughter in exchange for a guilty plea. Krotine would only have served 3 to 10 years.

"The main reason I said no was I knew, if I took a plea deal, they would stop looking for my wife's killer," he says.

Krotine says he knows who murdered Ramona, thanks to the work of Chris Giannini, a private investigator hired by his lawyers for the second trial.

Witnesses say a man named Robert Cameron danced with Ramona Krotine the night she disappeared. A handyman who lived in Lakewood, Cameron was employed by Sam Mazzola during the I-X Center's sports-and-outdoor show in March 2003. The two ran an exhibit that offered photographs taken with live bears and tigers. Mazzola says they attended the hotel party together at the end of the week.

As Mazzola left that night, he recalls, he offered Cameron a ride. It was late, and he knew that Cameron relied on public transportation. But he declined. The next day, Cameron showed up for work with long scratches on his head and hands, according to Mazzola.

Cameron said he was mugged at an RTA stop by "three niggers."

Mazzola suspected Cameron was lying. When Ramona's body was found later that day, his suspicions escalated.

Giannini describes Cameron as an ex-con who is "deep for trouble." He was busted for passing bad checks in 1991 and pleaded to felony theft in Lorain County in 1992. In 1997, his ex-wife filed for a restraining order, accusing him of domestic violence. At the time of Ramona's murder, his house was in foreclosure.

Ray Boyle, who operated a fence-building company with Cameron in 2002, hasn't seen him since then. Boyle says he ended their relationship after equipment and money went missing.

Cameron moved four times in 2003 before Giannini lost track of him.

"He's a scumbag drifter," Mazzola says. "He knew she was carrying $4,000 that night. He stole from friends of mine too. He knew everybody's business."

Mazzola and a friend were talking about Ramona's murder a couple of months later, when Cameron joined the conversation. "He told me that he got a ride from the hotel to the RTA station from Ramona that night," remembers Mazzola. "I looked at him and said, 'You killed her, didn't you?' I told him I would go to police."

Mazzola shared his story with Brook Park Detective William Lambert prior to the first trial. He was stunned by the response.

"He said he was going to charge me with perjury," he claims. "He said he wanted blood samples to see if *I* was at the crime scene." Detective Lambert and the Brook Park Police Department declined comment on Cameron and Mazzola.

Mazzola didn't volunteer his help to either side in the three trials. "I finally got to the point where I said, 'I don't know Jeff. I don't owe him anything. I can't do this anymore,'" he says. "I was done with it."

Krotine's defense never called Cameron to testify. In a conversation with Giannini, Cameron denied that Ramona had given him a ride.

"We didn't call him, because he wouldn't help us," says Michael Peterson, one of Krotine's lawyers in the third trial.

According to prosecutors, no evidence directly linked Cameron

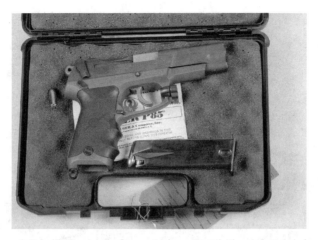

Jeffery Krotine kept a 9 mm sidearm at work, the same type of weapon that killed his wife, but prosecutors could not prove it was the one that shot Ramona. *(Cuyahoga County Coroner's Office)*

to Ramona's car. An arrest on an unrelated charge seemed to discredit Mazzola's claim.

"We have a booking photo from a week later, when he got into a fight at an RTA station," says Assistant Prosecutor Zimmerman. "There are no markings, no scratches on his head." And it shows that it's not out of Cameron's character to go fisticuffs with people at bus stops.

Cameron sued Mazzola in 2004, claiming he had been injured by the hood of Mazzola's truck while filling the oil tank but abruptly dropped the suit later that year.

"That was his way of getting back at me for going to police," says Mazzola.

Reached at his home in Vermilion, Cameron referred all comment to his lawyer, Michael Duff. "He had absolutely nothing to do with this. The defense created this as a red herring, something to confuse the jury with," Duff says.

To this day, Cameron has never explained why he never filed a police report if he really did get jumped at the RTA station the night Ramona died.

•   •   •

Plain Dealer headlines. *(Cleveland State University Archives)*

Krotine believes that Cameron killed his wife. But he insists the man was no more than a pawn—a hired gun in a sweeping conspiracy that implicates Krotine's longtime employer as well as the prosecutors who tried to put him away.

Krotine maintained a tense relationship with State Farm that went back at least to 1997, when, he says, local agents were asked to sign new contracts that would reduce their commissions on auto policies. Krotine was offered a substantial buyout, but with his long list of clients, he figured he would be better off not signing. He believes State Farm has had it in for him ever since.

His paranoia escalated in the fall of 2001, when one of his employees, Trese Huber, defected to another State Farm agency, taking many of her clients with her. The following year, Krotine lashed out, filing a $4.5-million civil suit against Huber and State Farm for violating its own noncompete clause.

At this point, Krotine's theory veers sharply beyond mere legal squawking. Facing his lawsuit and still paying him the higher commission, State Farm figured it would be cheaper to hire a hit man and frame Krotine for Ramona's murder, Krotine believes.

"The whole point was to take me out of the picture," he says.

Not surprisingly, Krotine's alleged co-conspirators are taken aback by his theory.

"That's so patently ridiculous we don't even want to comment on it," State Farm spokesman Phil Supple wrote in an e-mail. (CEO Ed Rust Jr. declined comment.)

"He's a sick man," says Trese Huber, who still works for State Farm. "I don't want to be in his path."

"This guy has gone off the deep end," Zimmerman says of Krotine. "The story is just so ridiculous, it demonstrates how desperate he is to point the finger at anyone else. He knows he did this, and it weighs on him every day."

Technically, the case is still open. But Brook Park Police say they already got their man.

Krotine's own lawyers cringe at the notion of a State Farm conspiracy. "I think he's a good man at heart," allows Michael Peterson. "He's just bizarre."

Krotine's suit against State Farm was dismissed in 2004. He remains insured by the company. Though he has never owned a boat, Krotine joined the Edgewater Yacht Club in 2001, when he was still a wealthy State Farm agent. In 2005, he shelled out $4,000 from his savings to be reinstated. They took his money, but he doesn't feel welcome. People talk behind his back, he says, trying to find a way to force him out.

But he takes solace in regaining a small piece of his old life: the wind drifting off Lake Erie, the view of the towers of Cleveland in the distance. And he's returned to selling insurance, as well. "I don't really know how to do anything else," he says.

He still sees Mary Engel, although the two say they're just friends. His children go on with their own lives apart from him, the relationship made more complicated by the lingering presence of the other woman.

"It seems like he's made his choice. We asked him not to come around anymore," says Jeff Jr. "This thing has totally ripped our family apart." Jennifer and Jason Krotine deferred to their older brother for comment.

Technically, Ramona's case is still open. But Brook Park Police say they already got their man.

"We stand by our investigation," says Chief Kevin McQuaid. "The evidence pointed only one way."

Another detective, who spoke on the condition of anonymity, puts it more bluntly: "What's frustrating is, we know who did it, and now there's nothing we can do. I hoped the family would sue him for wrongful death, but they just want to put it behind them. And I don't blame them, I guess. The jury expected more. We got screwed by *CSI*. People expect concrete evidence linking a murderer to a crime, but that doesn't usually happen like it does on TV."

There's one thing we can be certain of: Jeffrey Krotine is guilty of being a strange man. And that's no crime. But because Brook Park police and Cuyahoga County prosecutors have been so vocal about their personal opinions of his culpability, he will likely serve out the remainder of life in a prison of sorts, anyway; a world where most people he meets remember his name and associate it with doubt and suspicion. Nine out of ten people who meet with him to set up an insurance policy walk out the door as soon as they realize who they're dealing with, he says.

But Krotine does agree with police and prosecutors on one point. *Somebody* got away with murder.

Anyone with information related to the crime can contact Brook Park detectives at 216-433-1239.

CHAPTER 8

The Battle of Shaker Heights

The Unsolved Murder of Lisa Pruett

The young nurse became fascinated with the accused murderer during long shifts inside the mental ward. A hesitant friendship formed over games of chess, where he was the teacher and she was the student. But all that ended, according to her, with a confession of sorts.

This was in the fall of 1990. Anna (name changed to protect anonymity) had just graduated from Cleveland State University and was anxious to get a full-time job at a Northeast Ohio mental health facility to put her clinical psychology degree to use. She accepted a part-time position at Laurelwood, a prestigious hospital on the East Side where some of Cleveland's more notable families seek help for their troubled loved ones. She worked in the stabilization unit, where the most violent and deranged clients were kept, the unit with the "rubber rooms." Her job was to check patients' vital signs, write reports on their mental status, and search rooms for sharp objects and other contraband. Administrators promised her she would soon be offered a full-time job, if things worked out.

And so Anna didn't complain—at first—when managers assigned her an ever-changing array of shifts. There was no set schedule for her. On any given day, she might work morning, afternoon, or night. It wore on her. But it also gave her a unique perspective on the people staying at Laurelwood.

She noticed one young man who often wandered the halls, late at night. He seemed out of place. He didn't take medication like the other patients. He didn't wear a wrist band like the other patients. He didn't participate in group therapy. All he really did was play chess.

"The first time I saw Kevin, he was cool as a cucumber, playing chess in a room full of completely out-of-hand people," Anna told a Shaker Heights detective, in an interview two years later.

Tressler walked across the room to Kevin Young, the 18-year-old sitting in front of the chessboard, and asked him if he could teach her how to play. He was defensive, at first, almost paranoid. When he realized all she wanted was to learn the game, he calmed down, and began to teach her the basics.

Over the course of the next several days, Anna used chess as a means to communicate with Kevin, to get him to open up to her. Their conversations began innocently enough—*what sort of CD player should I buy, Kevin?*—but quickly led to more personal topics. He wanted to tell her about the pain he felt when he was rejected by girls at school. And, in return, she told him stories about her romantic relationships on the outside. He suggested they get together when he finally got out.

Then, one evening, she and Kevin and several other patients were watching the nightly news when the account of a local crime—the unsolved murder of Lisa Pruett—began. Kevin Young's picture appeared on screen, as the named suspect in the teenager's death. A couple of people in the room gasped. Kevin got up and walked away.

She gave him a few minutes, then went to his room. He said he didn't want to talk about it and asked her to leave.

Anna didn't bring the subject up again. The next day, it was as if nothing had happened. Their games of chess resumed. And so did their increasingly personal banter. He wanted to know who she was dating and how it was going for her.

In Loving Memory of Lisa Pruett

"My little girl, teach me to laugh again
Run in the wind and tumble in the grass again
When you're so alive and running by my side
Then you teach me to laugh, my little girl."

May 29, 1974 — September 14, 1990

". . . and I'll always remember you like a child,
girl. . ."

Cat Stevens

Classmates dedicated the 1990–1991 yearbook
to Lisa. *(Shaker High School yearbook)*

Towards the end of October, during another game of chess, according to Anna, he casually said to her, "They think I killed the little girl."

Anna didn't know how to respond. If he was talking about Lisa Pruett, who was 16 at the time of her murder, she thought it very odd of him to refer to her as a "little girl."

As media attention on Lisa's murder grew into a frenzy not seen in Cleveland since the Sam Sheppard case, Kevin became increasingly withdrawn and depressed. He mumbled to himself in Anna's presence. "I didn't mean to hurt the little girl, I didn't mean to hurt the little girl," he said, according to Anna.

One night, his percolating anger finally burst through. As Anna described it, Kevin stalked off from the common area and headed for his room in a huff. She didn't know what had caused him to react that way. She followed him down the hall. "Well, maybe I did hurt the little girl, maybe I did do it," she heard him say. Then, he punched the wall, hard.

"It was like he was a different person than he had been and it was a scary person," Anna would tell police. "I think I never believed up to that point that he was capable of such violence, but that night that did it for me."

That was the end of their friendship. A short time later, Anna quit her job at Laurelwood.

Like Tressler, many residents of Shaker Heights still believe Kevin Young killed Lisa Pruett, even though he has been acquitted of that crime.

But a closer look at the testimony and evidence—some of which was never presented in the trial or leaked to the press—tends to support the belief that the real killer was never indicted.

September 13, 1990, was the happiest day of Lisa Pruett's life. That's what the 16-year-old told her close friends. Each successive moment seemed filled with more good news and joy than the one before.

Lisa had a lot of friends at Shaker Heights High School. She was a fairly popular teen, smarter than the majority of her peers, with a sharp wit and a love of poetry. She was not eye-catchingly attractive, as were some of her upper-crust, salon-scene female classmates— daughters of doctors and lawyers and politicians—but she had a great smile and a curvy figure that did not go unnoticed. She was involved in a litany of extracurricular activities that included being a member of student council, leading a marching band squad, pitching for the JV softball team, playing field hockey, and writing for the *Shakerite*, the school paper. She also contributed this poem for the student lit magazine, *Semanteme*:

> *Flitting, floating, falling on the ground.*
> *I freeze on children's eyelashes, and blur*
> *their altered vision of the world.*
> *They see a different earth than I.*

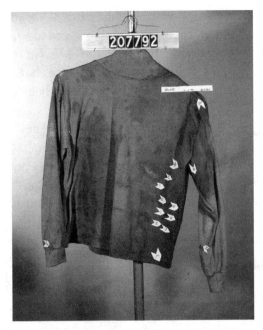

This coroner's photograph shows where the knife punctured her sweater. Her death was very violent. *(Cuyahoga County Coroner's Office)*

Of candy and playgrounds and eternal smiles.
I see the truth.
Cold bare trees, stripped of life and
hard ground.

In her writing, Lisa reveals a certain sadness, a longing to see the world with a little more optimism than she was ever allowed to possess. At 16, she knew that even in the safest communities, tragedy sometimes seeks you out. Her little brother, Brian, had died when he was only one year old, the victim of a fatal heart defect.

That Thursday, September 13, Lisa had an appointment to get her driver's license. She was older than many of her friends and had promised to be the chauffeur of the group, if they agreed to behave in the car. She only wished her boyfriend could be there to congratulate her in person, when she got back.

His name was Dan Dreifort, and the teenage boy was a bit of a rebel at Shaker High . . . as much of a rebel as a band nerd who lived in a mansion could feign to be, anyway. He was fan of alternative rock when R.E.M. was big and Nirvana had yet to change the world with *Nevermind.* He formed a band of his own called "Your Mother and Her Howling Commandoes." They practiced inside the basement of Dan's house, in a wing he referred to as "the Howling Commando room." At school, he got into some hot water with the principal after he and his friends starting walking the hallways, wearing single black gloves, and calling themselves "The Black Glove Cult." He liked to get high on cough syrup, too, a habit he picked up at church camp and introduced to his buddies back home. He hosted "Robo parties" at his house, where everyone drank Robitussin and listened to music.

> Lisa told every-one she bumped into that this was the best day of her life.

Dan had known Lisa for years, but on April 3, 1990, they fell deeply in love during a trip to Germany with the high school band. Lisa saw the good in Dan. At school, she wrote him notes the length of novellas. She shared with him her "Happy Book," a scrapbook in which she collected newspaper headlines and stories that made her smile. Sometimes, she recorded her voice for him, on cassette tapes, which he listened to whenever they were apart. Eventually, their love became physical. Dan was her first. And her first true love.

But on September 13, Dan had been away for over a month. He was on an extended vacation of sorts, on leave from school and Shaker Heights. Sent away by his father. In that month, Lisa had only seen him briefly, a couple of times, and anxiously awaited the day they would be reunited.

Was she surprised then, when Dan returned to Shaker Heights that very day? You bet. It was all she could talk about the rest of the day. She promised to come by Dan's house after flute lessons later that evening. They even made clandestine plans for Lisa to sneak out of her house after bed and ride her bike over to Dan's so that they could see each other again. Lisa told everyone she bumped into that this was the best day of her life.

. . .

Kevin Young was not having a good day. But every day seemed like a bad day to Kevin, each filled with more grief and disappointment than the last. He was looking forward to starting his freshman year at Ohio State University the following week, but he was worried his new life there might be just another misadventure waiting to happen.

On this particular day, he was obsessing over news that a former classmate had been deployed to the Middle East after Iraq invaded Kuwait. He worried the government would soon reinstate the draft.

Kevin's narcissistic fears often got the better of him. On a band trip to Toronto in 1988, he had threatened to jump from his hotel balcony because a girl had refused to break up with her boyfriend to go out with him. They called his father to come pick him up and he was placed in the mental unit at Hanna Pavilion upon his return. Doctors prescribed strong meds, which he was encouraged to continue taking. Kevin, however, complained the medication made him feel strange, so his parents allowed him to quit taking the pills in October 1989.

To look at a picture of him from back then, you'd never think Kevin would have had trouble getting a date. He was a handsome young man, with a crisp haircut and dark bangs that reached out over his eyes. But when he opened his mouth, more often than not, what came spilling out was hate and prejudice. He often ranted about blacks and Jews and how they were ruining Shaker Heights.

Usually, if you wanted to find Kevin Young, all you had to do was stop by the coffee shop Arabica in Shaker Square. There, he could play chess against *good* players. Sometimes grandmasters such as Calvin Blocker, an East Side eccentric who can challenge a hundred players simultaneously, would even drop in for a game or two. Kevin was no grandmaster in 1990, but he was well on his way, able to see seven moves ahead and anticipate his opponents' strategies.

That's where he was on September 13. All day.

A little after 10 P.M., a friend of Kevin's named Ken Workman

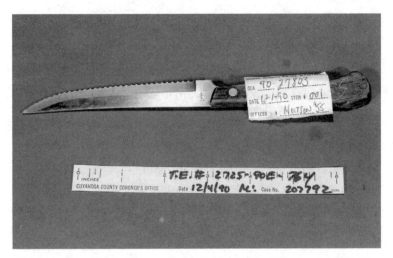

The coroner's office tested many knives to determine if they were used to kill Lisa. The murder weapon has not been found. *(Cuyahoga County Coroner's Office)*

came by. "Tex," as everyone called Ken, and Kevin had become blood brothers the previous year, swearing allegiance to each other as they cut fingers and pressed them together. Tex was dating Deb Dreifort, Dan's sister. But she had already left for Ohio University. Tex was 16 and still enrolled at Shaker Heights High School but often played hooky. He was on probation, at the time, for truancy, among other things.

Kevin and Tex sat at a table inside Arabica and talked for about 45 minutes. Tex told Kevin that Dan was planning to host one of his famous Robitussin parties later that night. He told Kevin that Lisa was coming around 12, 12:30, and so was another classmate named Chris Jones. Tex was planning on spending the night at the Dreifort's, too. But an invitation wasn't being extended to Kevin. Not that Kevin expected one. He knew he was an outsider.

At around 10:45 P.M., they paid their bills and went their separate ways. Kevin walked down Drexmore Road, a logical route back to his house on Onaway Road. Tex pedaled down Shaker Boulevard toward the Dreifort house on Lee Road.

·   ·   ·

Almost no one at Shaker High knew that Dan had spent 35 days inside the psych ward at Cleveland Clinic that fall. Not even Dan's closest friends knew that he, like Kevin, had suicidal tendencies (ideation, they're called) and required medication. But the extended stay didn't seem to be helping much. On a short leave from the Clinic at the end of August, he overdosed on antihistamines. His sister and Tex had called poison control.

On September 13, Dan was finally discharged from the clinic at 2 P.M. His father picked him up and they returned home, where Dan unpacked. Around 3 P.M., Dan rode his bike to the high school to surprise Lisa. He found her studying chemistry with Kim Rathbone, who lived in the house directly behind Dan's. Before Lisa, Dan and Kim had been an item and they were still close, often talking through the fence that separated their properties—or by phone—until late at night. Within minutes of his arrival, more of Dan's friends sought him out to welcome him back with hugs. Eventually, he escorted Lisa to her mom's car.

As soon as Dan got home, Kim came over. The house was empty—his parents weren't due home until after 5 P.M. They sat out on the back porch and talked. Kim wanted Dan to return some of the mementos she'd sent him at the clinic to cheer him up, little treasures that reminded her of him. Dan asked Kim to cut his hair before she left.

"Do whatever you want to," he told her, according to police reports. "I have complete faith in you."

At 6 P.M., Dan ate dinner with his parents, then helped his dad load logs into the back of the family van, wood from a tree which had fallen in a recent storm. Sometime around 8 P.M., Tex showed up. They sat on the porch and BS'd while Dan strummed a guitar. A little after nine, Lisa and her father pulled into the driveway and Lisa got out to talk with Dan. She couldn't stay long—her father had agreed to bring her by for only a couple of minutes after her evening flute practice. Lisa's father remained in his car in the driveway while Lisa and Dan walked around the corner of the house, where they kissed and talked in private for a few minutes. When they came back, they were talking about Dan's hair.

"I want to cut *your* hair," Dan told Lisa, according to Tex. He had clippers in one hand. "And I want Tex to hold you down while I do it."

Lisa told Dan that she was going to sneak out of her house and come back around 12 or 12:30. Friends named Chris Jones and Becca Boatright were going to do the same.

> **Although it looked like a sex crime at first, the coroner later determined she had not been raped.**

Then, Lisa left and Dan's mother told him that Tex had to leave. Instead, Tex offered to ride Dan's bike to Shaker Square to pick up some smokes (that's when Tex saw Kevin Young). Tex returned with the cigarettes around 11 P.M. He told Dan he was going home; he didn't know Chris Jones and didn't really want to sit around watching Dan and Lisa make out. So he walked toward the Rapid stop at the corner of Lee and Shaker Boulevard.

At 11:30 P.M., Dan went to his room and put on some music—a live performance of R.E.M., recorded in Holland on October 12, 1987. Around midnight, his sister Deb called from school. Dan's father talked to Deb on the master bedroom phone while his wife picked up the phone in the next room. Dan stood at the foot of his father's bed listening, adding to the conversation when needed. When their parents were done, Dan spoke to Deb alone, using the phone in the adjacent den.

At 12:15, according to his father, Dan returned to his bedroom.

Fifteen minutes later, the screaming began. The screams were Lisa's. She lay dying, in the neighbor's yard, 30 feet from Dan's house. She had been stabbed 21 times with a knife-like object. By the time police got there, she was dead. Her blue jeans and underwear had been pulled down and off her left leg. Her dark blue turtleneck had been pulled up over her bra. Although it looked like a sex crime at first glance, the coroner later determined she had not been raped. There were bruises on her neck that might have been caused by her necklace, if someone had pulled on it from behind. Her open eyes stared blankly back toward Dan's house.

• • •

"Could you describe what you remember of the screams that you heard?" the detective asked Dan Dreifort early the next morning at the Shaker Heights police station. He had just been read his rights and told he was a suspect in the aggravated murder of his girlfriend.

"It sounded like someone, a female, was being forced to do something that they didn't want to do, and it lasted for at least fifteen seconds, I don't know for sure," he answered.

Dan told police he had forgotten Lisa was coming over to meet him that night. After he spoke with his sister on the phone, he said, he had gone back to his room and was tidying things up when he heard the scream. The time was about 12:30 P.M.

"Was there a pause in the screaming, or was it a continuous scream?" the detective asked.

"Many short screams," Dan said.

Dan told the detective that he went to his window, which looked out over Lee Road, pulled the shade and tried to see where the screams were coming from. At that moment, he claims, his father cried out, "Did you hear that?" from his bedroom. Their bedrooms were connected by a bathroom. Dan opened his window. By the time the screams stopped, Dan was in his parents' room, according to their statements.

"My first inclination was to run outside and see what happened," said Robert Dreifort. "Realizing I was stark naked, I quickly looked at Dan to determine if he was more fully clothed than I." In fact, Dan was fully dressed. "I then noticed that he was wearing a pair of brown moccasins. This was important to me because I knew that he could get out quicker than me."

According to Dan and his father, at this point Dan ran outside to the front lawn, looking toward the corner of Lee and South Woodland, where the scream had seemed to originate. Dan's father, dressed now, arrived at the door. They both told police they couldn't see anything out of the ordinary, so they came back inside.

"I then went back to bed and began to read my book," said Robert.

Dan said he returned to his bedroom and continued to clean it. It was only then, he claimed, that he remembered Lisa was supposed to come over.

"At that point, did you think that the screams that you heard might possibly have been from Lisa?" the detectives asked.

"No," said Dan. "I didn't think that for a couple of minutes, but then I thought it might have been her."

He went back outside, he said, alone, and discovered Lisa's bike hidden in the bushes beside the sidewalk at his neighbor's house, at the corner of Lee and South Woodland.

"Then I ran home, called her house, got the answering machine, then called 911."

The police had already responded to a call from Dan's neighbors, about a scream originating near the corner of Lee and South Woodland. A cruiser had driven by at 12:35 P.M., but the officer had seen and heard nothing. When the police returned after Dan's 911 call, Dan was standing in the driveway of his house, waiting for them. He had not told his parents that he had called them.

"Why not?" asked the detective.

"I was too busy calling and running around," Dan said. "I wasn't thinking straight. I was in a rush."

When the policeman asked Dan if his parents knew that Lisa was supposed to come over that night, he said, "Yes" even though, later, both parents would deny being aware of their late-night rendezvous.

As the police officer searched the area, Dan went back inside, woke his father, who walked outside to talk to the officer. Then, according to Dan, while police searched for his missing girlfriend, without having notified Lisa's parents that anything was wrong, he went back to his room and went to sleep.

In that first interview, Dan did not mention to detectives that Chris Jones and Becca Boatright had been invited to his house that night. He didn't mention the Robo party. He told them about Tex, but didn't tell them that Tex had borrowed his bike to go to Shaker Square for smokes, information that would have been useful at the time.

• • •

Killer cuts down Shaker girl, 16

Pruett suspect's bond $50,000

Prosecutor asked judge to deny bail

By JAMES F. McCARTY
PLAIN DEALER REPORTER

CLEVELAND
Kevin Young, the preppy house painter charged with stabbing to death a former high school classmate, pleaded not guilty to the crime yesterday and was released from jail on $50,000 bond.

Jail a short while later after his parents put up their $300,000 house as collateral for the bail.

Marino, in arguing for continued incarceration, said Young had a "history of erratic behavior," including recent incidents in which Young was suspected of being unnaturally obsessed with two female students from Case Western Reserve University. The women complained to police, but no arrests were made, Marino said.

Marino said he planned to renew

Pruett case witness: 'I asked him if he killed her; he said yes'

By ULYSSES TORASSA
PLAIN DEALER REPORTER

CLEVELAND
Key evidence against Kevin Young, accused of the stabbing death of Lisa Pruett, was put on display yesterday, including a witness who said Young admitted saying the

month's trial, prosecutors Thursday brought some of their witnesses into Cuyahoga County Common Pleas Court to try to persuade a judge to open the records from Young's stay in an exclusive psychiatric clinic. The 18-year-old Ohio State University students circled into Laurel-

mitted to several law problems, rather than for legitimate therapy.

Three of Young's fellow patients at Laurelwood took the stand yesterday, and each said the young man have participated in any of the ordinary therapy programs at bush intimation like the other patients.

One woman, Martha Helen Hranz,

encounter in one of the lounge areas. Later a lot of first meetings. She only out of why he was there came up as part of an ordinary small-talk, she said.

"He take me his father wanted her there to keep Lisa from the police," she said. "He said that was because he was accused of of killing someone," M. Marino.

When she asked for details Young

with numerous clippings about the Sept. 12, 1990 Pruett murder, Hranz said.

"I asked him if he killed her," Hranz said.

"He said, 'Yes'," she said.

Verdict left jurors frustrated

Suspected they hadn't heard full story about Kevin Young

By JAMES F. McCARTY

of the jury agreed to acquit Kevin Young of the murder of Lisa Pruett

They never heard from the woman at Case Western Reserve University

Judge James J. Sweeney was never asked to decide the admissibil-

Plain Dealer headlines. *(Cleveland State University Archives)*

The only person who mentioned Kevin's name, on record, to detectives on Friday, the first day of the investigation, was Tex, and Tex did not mention he had told Kevin that Lisa was coming over. In Tex's first statement, Kevin is only mentioned in passing, as a friend he bumped into at Arabica. Kevin Young became interesting to detectives only after a discussion that took place at Dan's house Friday night, between Dan, his sister Debbie, and Chris Jones.

According to Chris's statement, he had decided not to go to Dan's house the evening of the murder because he was working on a paper for school. He had spent most of the night at fencing practice and had to work on the paper until midnight to get it done.

The next day, Chris was at Dan's house when the evening news came on at 5 P.M. TV reporters hinted that Dan was the prime suspect in the murder and this upset Dan, he told the police.

At some point that evening, Chris left Dan's house with two friends—Dan Messinger and Scott Fiero. Messinger and Chris were dropped off at Lisa's house, where they "spent a little time in Lisa's room." Chris returned to the Dreifort residence and spent the night there. Sometime that evening, he and Dan and Debbie went downstairs, to the Howling Commando room, to talk about the murder.

"We discussed the possibility that Kevin Young might have done it," Chris later told detectives. "It started from Shane [McGee] and John [George] who had heard about a month before that Kevin had wanted to kill both Dan and Lisa because he had been in love with Lisa for two years, and Dan had stolen her away from him." They also discussed this idea with Becca Boatright.

The supposed threats were never reported, though, until the next day, September 15, when Shane and John went to the Shaker Heights police and repeated these statements to detectives.

"Somebody told Kevin that Dan had had sex with Lisa and Kevin went nuts," said Shane. "He got very aggressive, both his language and physically, it was obvious he was distraught. He said he wanted to kill Dan and launch war on the female race. In some context he said that he wanted to kill Lisa and Dan Dreifort. I can't remember the exact wording he used, but he was very clear about his meaning."

"I said, 'He's sleeping with her,' and Kevin just freaked," said John. "He was like, 'That asshole, that asshole, I hate him. I'm going to kill him. I want her dead,' then he stormed off and left me and Shane."

If Tex had mentioned to police that he had told Kevin that Lisa was coming over to Dan's house, *before* Shane and John accused Kevin of threatening Lisa's life, it would seem a little less like they were trying to deflect the heat away from Dan and onto Kevin. But Tex only mentioned that Kevin knew Lisa was coming over in a *second* statement taken on September 17. Later, this statement was retyped into a standard police record. Somewhere along the line, and it's hard to tell if this happened at Shaker Heights police headquarters or in the offices of the county prosecutor, that new record of Tex's second statement—which he and his mother signed on September 17, 1990, in the presence of detectives—was erroneously dated: September 14.

·　　　·　　　·

Every friend of Dan's that police interviewed after the late night meeting in Dan's basement had nothing but damning things to say about Kevin Young.

Becca Boatright gave her statement on September 15. She told police that on the afternoon after Lisa's murder, she had gone to Arabica and found Kevin sitting there. "Somehow or other, I got onto the topic of rape," she said. The news broadcasts were reporting that first day that Lisa had probably been raped. "Kevin said, 'I don't think she was raped.' I told him that I had heard she . . . had been hit on the head with a blunt object. He said, 'No, I think she was stabbed.'"

A classmate named Jennifer Margulies told police she had been sitting with Kevin at Arabica when he found out that Dan was out of the hospital. "Kevin said, 'I have some unfinished business to take care of.'" Jennifer said she only realized Kevin was a suspect after she heard it from a friend of Becca's.

"[Kevin] said that he was gonna get Lisa," said Kim Rathbone, in her statement. "He's scary, but you never think that anybody's actually going to do something, even though they talk."

"Okay, so this is what you've heard from other people?" the detective asked.

"Yeah."

"Who has been talking to you about it?"

"Jennifer Margulies."

Kevin Young denied ever threatening Lisa Pruett when he was brought into the station after 11 P.M., on September 15. He said the conversation with Shane McGee and John George never took place. He said after leaving Shaker Square the night of the murder, he returned home. Both his mother and father saw him go to his room around 11:30 P.M. At 11:45 P.M., he went downstairs and watched CNN because he couldn't sleep.

But the detectives didn't believe him.

From the supplementary notes of Detective Richard Mullaney: "Later in the interview of Kevin Young, he was confronted with the fact that he was the one who had killed Lisa Pruett. At that point, Young became indignant and vehemently denied that he could be the one who did that." Kevin offered to take a polygraph to prove it. Instead, Detective Mullaney and his partner left him alone, to stew, while they observed him through a two-way mirror. "While Kevin was by himself, he became visibly intense and was taking deep drags on his cigarette. Young's eyes were watering heavily and at times, he would draw his legs up underneath himself on the chair while turning sideways, and assumed what could be described as the 'fetal' position. Also at this time, Young, on two different occasions, stared straight ahead with an intense look and mouthed the words, 'No, No, No,' very slowly and deliberately."

From this moment on, Kevin Young was the one and only suspect in the murder of Lisa Pruett in the minds of the detectives in charge of solving the case. They were particularly suspicious of inconsistencies in Kevin's statement that didn't jibe with the facts they already knew about the day of the murder. For example, Tex told Kevin about Dan's Robo party at Arabica, but Kevin told police that conversation had taken place at the Shack, a restaurant nearby. Kevin had met Tex at the Shack the next day.

"It was there [at the Shack that Tex] was accusing Dan of Lisa's murder," Kevin said. "He was threatening to kill Dan if he found out that Dan killed Lisa." According to Kevin, Tex also asked him to make sure the cops knew that they had been together until a quarter to 11, the night of the murder. Tex was worried that police wouldn't buy his alibi—that he had returned to Dan's and then walked to the rapid station, where he waited for 45 minutes for a bus. Tex had a knife which police might find if they searched the Dreiforts' house. Deb had taken the knife from Tex after he got busted for truancy and had to report to a probation officer, so that he wouldn't get himself in trouble for carrying a concealed weapon. But Tex had little reason to worry. His story checked out with the bus logs at the Regional Transit Authority, his mother said he was home before 12:30 P.M., Deb claimed she had taken the knife to school with her, and he passed a polygraph test.

Still, Kevin told police he had doubts. "I'm really worried that

Tex did this," he said. "I hope it's not true. But if he did this for me, because of a crush I had on Lisa, back around the time of the Germany trip, this will be on my conscience forever."

A search warrant was served at the Young's house on September 16. Curiously, police evidence logs erroneously list the date of this search as September 14, again giving the false impression that Kevin was a suspect before Dan's friends implicated him. What detectives found at Kevin's house, however, didn't help his case.

They found drawings of pentagrams; a devil face; a heart tattooed with a Christian cross, stabbed and dripping blood. And his diary wasn't that of a well-adjusted young man. "This is day one of my diary. My Mom is a bitch and I hate her. I'll explain tomorrow." And then: "I just want to take over the world. Make the blacks and Jews, and the Slavs and the Latins and the yellows and the Semites subordinate to us. I am worth absolutely nothing."

> Kevin Young was the only suspect in the minds of the detectives in charge of the case.

Detectives got samples of Dan's writing, too. Inexplicably, they did not seem as interested in them, even though they are much more explicit.

In a letter to Lisa during his stay at the Clinic, Dan wrote, "I tried to kill myself. I need out of here. This place has fucked me up. After I get out, give me some time to return to normal. I don't want you or I to make any poor decisions because of this place."

In a note to Lisa, Dan quoted lyrics to her. "I'm sorry now I killed you. For our love was something fine. And till they come to get me, I shall hold your hand in mine."

In another note to Lisa: "Some day, I'll go too far and do something very bad and you'll yell at me and be serious and I won't be able to handle it. But you can't let me get away with murder. I look at you and see what I've done to you. I'm a bad influence on people. Chris is another example of this. And believe it or not, I think I've made Kevin [Young] worse than he already was."

Another note: "I wanna poke your eyes out with my favorite pocket knife."

One letter ends, cryptically, with this code: IDTDODAFNDOT (H)KOBRT."

Detectives also pulled Tex Workman and Debbie Dreifort's phone records. They reveal that Tex called Debbie's dorm at 12:19 P.M. and the call lasted until 12:54 P.M. The records rule Tex out as a suspect, but they also increase the amount of time Dan was alone, prior to anyone hearing Lisa's screams.

But when detectives enlisted the help of trained psychiatrists, they were only interested in understanding one mental patient: Kevin Young.

On Monday, September 17, FBI Special Agent Dick Wrenn paid a personal visit to the Shaker Heights police detective bureau. At the time, Wrenn was the lead agent assigned to the unsolved murder of 10-year-old Amy Mihaljevic. Wrenn was anxious to see if there were any similarities between Lisa's murder and Amy's.

Shaker Heights police welcomed the assistance. After detectives read Kevin's diary, they called Wrenn and asked if there was someone inside the Behavioral Science unit at FBI who could offer an opinion on what it said about Kevin's nature. Wrenn recommended Special Agent James Wright, a profiler working out of the Academy at Quantico.

Wright told them, over the phone, that based on the diary, "Kevin Young has no ego, has low self esteem." His personality "definitely fit that of a person capable of committing the crime." He suggested that when detectives interviewed Kevin, again, for the polygraph, they should interview him at night, "the later the better," because Kevin was a night person. He warned the police not to be judgmental when they questioned him. That they should give him an "out" such as suggesting that maybe Kevin wasn't in control of himself when he murdered Lisa and therefore not responsible.

On September 25, Shaker Heights detectives and Special Agent John Dunn flew to Quantico to speak to Wright in person. Agent Wright and his staff described Kevin as a "John Hinckley" type personality, someone who fantasized about women from afar. They suggested he might be a serial killer. Again, they went over strategies for the upcoming polygraph interview: have pop and cigarettes on hand, be prepared to question him for hours before getting a confession, use a "third person" approach when talking about the crime.

Meanwhile, Kevin had moved into a dorm at Ohio State. He started taking classes and began to think maybe this whole thing was behind him. Then, on October 26, 1990, while he was on the phone with his father, there was a knock at the door. It was Shaker Heights Police Sergeant Tom Gray. Kevin told his dad that he would call him back.

Sergeant Gray usually worked with juveniles. He had the "soft approach" that the profiler said was needed to get Kevin to confess. And in his later report of that night, it's obvious Gray was not just playing good cop. Throughout the course of the long interrogation, Gray came to care for Kevin, even if he thought the young man was a cold blooded killer.

Before the polygraph was administered, Sergeant Gray spoke to Kevin, at length, inside a room at a Columbus hotel. On hand were plenty of cigarettes and soda.

At first, he let Kevin lead the conversation. They talked about the growing trouble in the Middle East and the threat of a draft. Gray told Kevin about how, when he was a teenager, he had to worry about the Vietnam draft. He listened while Kevin explained how Iraq could be saved using nonviolent economic means.

Then, Gray asked Kevin to put himself in the place of the person who killed Lisa and explain what he thought happened.

"Just between us?" asked Kevin.

"Yeah, just to kind of help me think through the thought process," Gray said.

Kevin told him that he thought Lisa had been riding her bike when the person grabbed her off the bike and it rolled into the bushes. He said that the person who did it didn't really think about it ahead of time. That he was just walking around that night and saw Lisa, and when she got close something snapped. Kevin said that he was sure that whoever did it would never kill again because he was so scared when Lisa died, that he couldn't do it again.

It seemed like a confession. But when Gray pushed for more details that only the killer would know, Kevin couldn't help him. Still pretending to think like the killer, Kevin told him that the man probably stabbed Lisa from the front just a couple of times. But Lisa was stabbed mostly from behind, a total of 21 times.

Gray tried to turn up the heat by implying the police had evidence against him, which they did not actually have. "Is there any reason we might find your fingerprints on Lisa's jeans?" he asked.

Kevin told him to take his fingerprints, if that's what he believed. He said there was no way his prints could be on Lisa's clothes. He said again that he would take a polygraph, if they didn't believe him.

It was 2 A.M. by the time Kevin was strapped into the lie detector in an adjacent room of the hotel. Polygraph expert Tom Kohanski asked Kevin the following questions:

1. Do you know for sure who killed Lisa?
2. The person who killed Lisa, do you know their first name?
3. The person who killed Lisa, do you know where they live?
4. When Lisa was killed, were you there?
5. The weapon used to kill Lisa, did you throw it away?
6. Did you ever hurt Lisa?
7. Did you kill Lisa?

In Kohanski's professional opinion, the results of questions 1 and 4 were inconclusive. On all the other questions, he found "minor deception." He told Sergeant Gray that Kevin seemed fatigued and should rest before being questioned again. So Gray let Kevin sleep. But the interrogation wasn't over.

In the early afternoon, Gray treated Kevin to lunch at a nearby Pizza Hut. They split a pepperoni pie and talked about college life. When they got back, Kevin returned to the polygraph room with Kohanski and took two more tests. Kohanski left the room this time to talk to Sergeant Gray.

He told Gray that Kevin showed deception on most of the questions dealing with Lisa's murder. Kohanski had even confronted

Kevin about this, and Kevin had started crying. "I didn't do it," Kevin had said. Gray returned to the room to talk to his suspect.

"I told Kevin that I had enjoyed the time with him but that it had been a long day and that I had to get back to the real world," writes Gray in his notes. "I told Kevin he had to get back to the real world, too. I told him that until this was resolved he couldn't go back to Shaker because everybody in Shaker would think of him as being a suspect. I told him he couldn't go back until he told the truth. Kevin reacted. He looked me right in the eyes, and with tears welling up in his eyes and deep emotion in his voice, he said he could have told me he did it, spent a couple years in a hospital, then got on with his life. But, he said, 'I've got to tell you the truth.'"

> *At the urging of his lawyer, Kevin took another lie detector test. This time, Kevin passed.*

Then, according to Gray, Kevin said, "I am scared. I feel suicidal. I have nothing to live for." He said he wanted to be hospitalized. Gray told Kevin he should call his parents, but Kevin called his doctor, instead. The doctor agreed to commit Kevin, but only if he talked to his parents, first, for insurance purposes. And so Kevin called home to discover that police had executed another search warrant there during his interrogation. His mother put Kevin in touch with their attorney, and the interview was over.

"Kevin, with tears in his eyes, asked if this meant I couldn't visit him in the hospital," Gray wrote in his report. "I simply told him that he needed to make those arrangements with his parents and attorney. He gave me a hug as we waited for the elevator."

That night, Kevin was admitted into Laurelwood hospital, where he remained for two months.

At the urging of his lawyer, Kevin took another lie detector test, administered by renowned expert Bill Evans (who has been used by both prosecutors and defense lawyers). This time, Kevin passed. The method used by Shaker Heights had been "debunked" in 1982, according to Kevin's attorney.

•   •   •

Even with a "failed" polygraph test, the Shaker Heights police department could not get the prosecutor's office to take their circumstantial case to a grand jury. While they waited, Kevin's name was leaked to the media as the main suspect in Lisa's murder. And when reporters discovered that Kevin's father, J. Talbot Young, was a law partner of Steve Alfred, the mayor of Shaker Heights, all hell broke loose. Reporters implied that the mayor had called in a favor for his friend. They suggested the Youngs were hiding Kevin inside the mental unit at Laurelwood. Investigative mug Carl Monday staked out Kevin's house, waiting for him to return.

When Kevin was finally released from Laurelwood on December 12, the media frenzy kicked into high gear. No one could understand why the police were not arresting this young man if every detective who spoke on the condition of anonymity said he did it. The city hired Wyse-Landau Public Relations to work damage control, and police detectives consulted with another psychiatrist to try to help them elicit a confession from Kevin before Shaker Heights ripped itself apart.

Detectives provided copies of Kevin's statements, interviews, writings, and polygraph results to Dr. Murray Miron, a professor of psychology at Syracuse University who frequently advised the FBI regarding the workings of the criminal mind. On June 11, Shaker Heights deputy chief James Brosius spoke with Miron, along with the university's chief of security, over the phone.

Miron: "You know, at some point the kid should have said, 'Hey, listen, I've answered all your questions. I can't go any more. Stop this nonsense.'"

Brosius: "We couldn't get him out of there."

Miron: (Laughs)

Brosius: "He just wouldn't leave."

Miron: "I might have been tempted at some point to say, 'You fucking bore me. Just go away, you bore me. I don't want to sit here and masturbate. When we want you, we'll come fetch you.' Our problem now of course, is he's represented by attorneys."

Miron suggested that Kevin suffered from multiple personality disorder, and was able to dissociate himself from the event of Lisa's murder. People with true dissociative personalities can beat lie detector tests, because they are able to fool themselves into believing the crime never occurred.

Miron: "Where are you with him right now? What's happened?"

Brosius: "Right now we're hung up with zero evidence. We haven't been able to put this kid on the scene."

Chief of Security: "Was he known to carry a knife?"

Brosius: "No. Everybody thinks he's kind of weird, well, we talked to the rest of the kids in this group. They're all weird. Even the girl's boyfriend was described by Jim Wright as sort of a paranoid schizophrenic, and he just got out of a mental institution the day of the murder."

Chief of Security: "The boyfriend did?"

Brosius: "Yeah."

Later, Miron hedges his opinions on Kevin, since he has not been able to view the material related to any other suspect.

Miron: "Understand, I've got a spread of one. You've given me no other suspects. The boyfriend, anything you have, please send that along just for the sake of completeness of the file, if nothing else. Until another suspect drops out of the sky, I'd say this is a logical suspect."

At this point, even Brosius seemed to question his opinions.

Brosius: "We're doing just as much investigation on Dreifort as we did on Young . . . and the parents could have fashioned this whole story about him coming and hearing the screams and grabbing him and going outside and all this kind of stuff, but I don't know . . ."

Miron: "Well, nobody said it was gonna be easy."

On July 17, 1991, after the Cuyahoga County prosecutor's office again refused to bring the evidence against Kevin in front of a grand jury, Shaker Height's law director, K.J. Montgomery, held a press conference. Hopefully, she wasn't following the advice of Wyse-Landau PR, because it didn't go well. Cleveland's godfather of journalism, Dick Feagler, blasted the city of Shaker Heights in an editorial commentary on Channel 3, later that night.

"Now, I've never seen anything like it so that makes it news to me," said Feagler. "Shaker Heights is up in arms, full of rumors, anger, unease, about who killed 16-year-old Lisa Pruett. Sleep well, they tell the citizens of Shaker Heights, the murderer is still at large. We know who he is, we just can't prove it. Well, the murderer of Lisa Pruett is still at large but whether Shaker Heights Police know who he is, is a matter of some dispute.

> *"Shaker Heights is up in arms, full of rumors, anger, unease, about who killed 16-year-old Lisa Pruett."*

"We know this much. We know that there is a young man who remains under a cloud because at an earlier press conference police indicated he was the prime suspect and leaked his name to the media. We know that police interrogated the young man for 18 hours without an attorney present, searched his room, gave him a lie test, and sent samples of his nails and skin to the FBI and came up with nothing. Not, as one lawyer put it, 'insufficient evidence,' no evidence.

"Yet, tonight, because of that press conference today, everybody who cares will be convinced that the young man is a murderer. No, I've never seen anything quite like it. It's easier than an arrest, it's cheaper than a trial. An interesting technique, but flawed because the murderer is still at large."

Deputy Chief Brosius followed up with Dr. Murray Miron on July 2. By then, Miron had had time to review some evidence related to Dan Dreifort and had some concerns regarding his behavior the night of the murder.

Miron: "[He] calls 911 on his own . . . and here are all these police vehicles, the crime scene being established . . . Dan goes to bed."

Brosius: "Right."

Miron: "I found that unusual . . . uh . . . somewhat disconcerting. But that's academic, because it's not Dan that we're going to be interrogating, it's Kevin, and whether or not he is the guy or not, we want to give the full shot . . . to use the best psychological coercion we can."

Miron went on to describe to police how to use psychological coercion to trick Kevin into confessing: "You take a mouse, a rat, and you want him to, let's say, twirl around three times clockwise in a sort of ballet-like pirouette. So what you do to control, is, you're in control over their reinforcements. You don't need to punish, but you can withhold the reinforcements, so what you do is you wait for the animal to turn its head and look to the right and then you give it a little bit of food."

Miron (later): "Now here's . . . forgive all the anecdotal sort of thing . . . we need to operant condition Kevin. *Clockwork Orange* on Kevin, if you've seen that film."

It would be another year and a half before Kevin was finally indicted.

Shaker Heights police got their indictment on November 24, 1992, after two patients from Laurelwood came forward, claiming Kevin had confessed to murder while inside the hospital's mental ward.

The first witness claimed Kevin had come to her in the hospital, one night, to show her newspaper clippings about Lisa's murder. "I asked him, 'Did you do it?'" she told police. "He said yes he did. I asked him why. His answer was, 'because.'" At the time of this "confession," Heinz was on a litany of psych meds, including lithium, Klonopin, and Depakote.

A second patient, also a client of lithium, said that Kevin told her, "You know that girl who was murdered? They'll never find out who killed that girl. There were only two people there; one of them is dead and the other will never talk."

Still, the prosecutor decided it was enough to charge Kevin with a single count of aggravated murder and face a maximum sentence of life in prison. Kevin's father hired Mark DeVan, one of the best defense attorneys in Cleveland, to represent his son. He immediately earned his retainer; when assistant county prosecutor Carmen Marino asked the judge to deny bail at Kevin's arraignment, DeVan successfully argued for a reduced bond of $50,000. Kevin's parents put up their home as collateral.

Prosecutors were dealt another blow when Judge James J. Sweeney refused to allow them to enter notes taken by Kevin's personal psychiatrist as evidence. Marino suggested to reporters that the notes could implicate Kevin in Lisa's murder.

In reality, there is nothing in the doctor's detailed and voluminous file that mentions a confession. When Kevin visited his doctor a day after Lisa's murder, Kevin wanted to talk about the possibility of being drafted into the Army, if there was a war in the Middle East. Lisa's murder was only mentioned in passing, because it was on the news.

The Youngs hired an expert from Texas named Robert Hirschhorn, whose sole job was to pick a perfect jury. He assisted DeVan in the voir dire process, where a pool of jurors is vetted by the defense and prosecution until twelve remain. This rubbed many blue-collar Clevelanders the wrong way, of course, and the media played it up grandly.

Kevin's trial began on June 28, 1993. It was broadcast nationally on Court TV. Edythe Heinz and Susan Lape were the prosecution's star witnesses.

It quickly became evident that the defense hoped to pin the murder on Dan Dreifort. And so DeVan had an attentive audience when he got the opportunity to question the boyfriend on the stand. The attorney asked him about the threatening letters he had sent to Lisa.

Dan said they were "harmlessly funny."

"That was your humor back then," asked DeVan.

"Yes it was. Lisa thought it was funny, too," said Dan.

When asked to explain why he went to sleep when police were outside, searching for his girlfriend, Dan said that sleep was his way of escape.

DeVan pounced. "Escape from something you knew about?"

"No," said Dan. "Escape from what I feared had happened."

"Did you in fact kill Lisa Pruett?" asked DeVan.

"No," said Dan.

Then, on July 6, DeVan unveiled a surprise: a statement by Edward Curtin, the police officer who was first to arrive on scene the night of the murder. Curtin said Dan had told him then that he had never heard the screams.

On July 17, Kevin's father, J. Talbot Young took the stand. He testified that at the time of the murder, he and Kevin were home, playing video games. According to Kevin's father, he had challenged Kevin to a Nintendo game after he had finished up work and found his son downstairs at the TV. They went to bed at 1:15 A.M.

On July 21, after 10 hours of deliberations, the jury found Kevin not guilty.

But that wasn't good enough for the press, who had been spoonfed information by Shaker Heights officials and prosecutors for years.

A week later, *Plain Dealer* reporter James F. McCarty wrote a feature article suggesting that jurors would have voted differently if they had gotten a chance to see evidence withheld by the judge. Kevin was devastated by the attack. That day, he climbed onto a bridge over Interstate 271 and threatened to jump. A Mayfield Heights police sergeant talked him down.

Kevin Young and his family are still fearful of the media, 15 years later. Who can blame them? I attempted to contact Kevin for this story. I spoke with Mark DeVan and his father, briefly, but, through them, Kevin decline an interview. He still haunts coffee shops in Shaker Heights and Coventry and works as a house painter.

"With Kevin Young, there was no smoking gun," admits Brosius, who left Shaker to become the police chief of Chagrin Falls. But, he's not interested in discussing other suspects.

Lisa's parents moved away from Shaker shortly after her murder but quietly returned to the area, recently. I spoke to her father at length, off the record. All official comments are still handled by the family's lawyer, Joseph Swartz. "It's been 19 years, but it's still very emotional for them," he says.

Dan Dreifort was harder to reach. His last listed number is the office of *Athens News*, an alternative weekly that serves the Ohio University campus, where Dan once worked as a graphics designer.

He is rumored to be living in New York City and playing in a new band. He called me one afternoon, after a friend passed along an interview request.

"I'll talk to you if Lisa's parents say it's okay," he told me. But after I got permission from Lisa's father, Dan decided to back out.

The Lisa Pruett murder remains an open and active case. Anyone with information can contact Shaker Heights detectives at 216-491-1261.

CHAPTER 9

A Killer Comes to Pancaketown

The Unsolved Murder of Dan Ott

The center of Burton, a bucolic village off Route 87 in Geauga County, is a patch of land with a log cabin that sells pure maple syrup year-round—hence the nickname "Pancaketown." But the heart of Burton is a firearms store. The Gunrunner is where everything happens. Everything of importance, anyway. Just ask the owner, Scott Weber.

"This is the epicenter, man. All the politics happen here. Deals are cut here. The mayor's been in here a bunch of times. We've done fundraising for [Congressman Steve] LaTourette. I know the sheriff real well. He comes in here to buy some shells. So I have an 'in.' So maybe he told me some things he wouldn't tell the regular newspaper guys."

In this case, the sheriff has been talking to Weber about a murder that happened down the road a stretch, in 2006. A vicious killing, not the sort of thing residents of Burton are used to. It's big news. Especially because the killer is still out there.

Weber is a singular soul with enough charisma to drown in. He has reddish-brown hair curled up in tufts around his noggin. He speaks in staccato flashes that are more like information downloads than actual conversation. And he has this habit of fidgeting with his thin copper-frame glasses while he prattles on. It's hard to get a word in edgewise, but it's amusing to try.

Sometimes, Weber's audacity gets him into trouble. In 2005, he posted his new *Girls of the Gunrunner* calendars on the storefront window for all to enjoy (the calendar ships with every gun you purchase and features buxom gals from the Cleveland area in skimpy clothing, posing with sidearms). After several complaints, the zoning board tried to shut him down, said there was simply too much material covering the windows—local law states that 50 percent of the window must be clutter-free. So Weber removed community flyers and advertisements, everything except the semi-nude women. The calendars covered only 45 percent of the window, so they had to let him keep them up.

Then, he launched BurtonBlog.com, a Web site on which he rants daily about life in Burton. When the town council proposed painting the water tower to resemble a stack of giant pancakes, Weber led the charge to nix the idea, opining on BurtonBlog that it would quickly become an eyesore. Council followed.

Weber knows how to craft an argument. He has a journalism degree from the University of Wyoming and taught the subject in high school for 25 years. Today his site gets 16,000 hits a month. When Weber blogs, people around here listen. And he has a lot to say about the murder that happened out on Claridon-Troy Road. Things some people don't want to hear.

He sits down on a green leather recliner near the back of the Gunrunner, beside a coffee table covered with old issues of *Stuff* magazine and *GQ*. Behind him is a row of shotguns tagged for auction. He gently removes his glasses from the bridge of his nose and fiddles with them like a bored kid.

"Here's the thing that strikes me as odd about this case . . ."

Dan Ott lived life on his own terms.

At Vermilion High School, Dan dated the superintendent's daughter. Daring, to be sure. But not as daring as the well-known

Blogger and gun shop owner Scott Weber has his own theories about the crime.

crushes he had for older, married women.

Ken Kishman, a friend of Dan's since the seventh grade, laughs, recalling Dan's unique confidence. "I remember him trying to pick up my girlfriend's mom," says Kishman. "He always kept in touch with his girlfriends' mothers."

Not that Dan was cocky, even if he had reason to be. In school, he excelled in art class; his friends still speak about his drawings and sketches with reverence 13 years later. There was a certain maturity in his brushstrokes. And in his life, too. He partied with his peers, but he didn't drink, didn't do drugs. Dan was fiercely intelligent and possessed this odd, intuitive sense for nature and how it operated.

Once, Kishman and Dan built a campfire on a cement patio behind the Ott residence. In the morning, they discovered the fire had singed part of the lawn. Dan took his knife over to the neighbor's yard, clipped a few inches where it wouldn't be missed, and transplanted the grass to where the damage had occurred. The new blades blended in perfectly.

"He could have been a brain surgeon," says Kishman. "He could have been anything." But Dan couldn't decide what he wanted to do.

After graduation, Dan announced that he was setting out for an extended hike. He told his friends he was walking across the country. He told his mother he just wanted to find the Appalachian Trail. He got about 30 miles from Vermilion before his bad knee, injured in high school track, got the better of him. Later, he hopped a bus to Chicago and explored the city for a couple of weeks before returning.

Back in Ohio, Dan took a job at Green Circle Growers in Kipton. He did grunt work at first, but over time, he was promoted to "grower." That's where Dan discovered he had a gift for cultivating seeds, nurturing them into healthy starter plants for customers. His name became known among Ohio's green-thumb community. He was respected in his field, scouted by Northeast Ohio greenhouses like some hotshot minor-league baseball player with a trick curve. No one could grow plugs like Dan Ott.

In 2003, Dan was hired by Urban Growers, a greenhouse on Claridon-Troy Road (State Route 700) in Burton Township. Part of the deal was that Dan could live in the small house next to the farm, rent-free. He was so good, competing greenhouses purchased Dan's plants from Urban Growers to sell in their shops.

"It's something not everyone can do," says Sue Herring, who worked with Dan at Urban Growers. "You have to understand pH balance, every little ingredient the plant needs and when it needs it. Me, I plant the seed. I'm a planter. But he was a *grower*." And he was just a nice guy. He liked to take Sue's mother out for ice cream now and then.

In 2006, a greenhouse in Michigan discovered Dan and offered him $30,000 more than what he was pulling in at Urban Growers. There was room for advancement, too; if he stayed on track, he could run his own greenhouse within two to three years, earning a six-figure salary. Dan accepted the offer but didn't leave in a hurry. He lingered in Burton, teaching his replacements how to grow seeds from old plants while slowly moving his things to Michigan. His first day at the new greenhouse would have been May 29, 2006.

Everyone who knew Dan Ott seemed to love him. Friends can't image who want to kill him.

Dan's live-in girlfriend, Maryann Ricker, was supposed to go with him.

Former co-workers say Dan met the 31-year-old hairdresser at a wedding and that they had been dating for more than a year. They liked to drive into town to see movies together. Although Dan wasn't a social drinker, the couple was often seen at Twisters, a local tavern that also serves food. She was the fair-looking blonde with dimpled cheeks and a constant smile. Dan was the easygoing guy with the bushy black goatee.

According to Maryann's statement to police, she and Dan slept on an air mattress on the living room floor the night of May 25. Almost everything had been moved to Michigan by then. All that remained, besides the makeshift bed, were some boxes and clothes. At about 6:30 the next morning, a Friday, Maryann says a man dressed in camouflage and a dark mask entered their home. He carried a shotgun.

The intruder ordered Maryann and Dan onto their stomachs. He bound Dan's wrists with duct tape, which Maryann says the intruder must have brought with him because she didn't remember having any in the house. Once the man moved to her, Dan managed to free himself from the tape and started to attack the armed stranger.

The masked man shot Dan in the chest and fled the scene. From the kitchen, she watched the man escape in a maroon Ford sedan.

At 6:35 A.M., Maryann called 911. Exactly what was said between the dispatcher and Maryann is unknown. The machine that tapes 911 calls at the Geauga County Sheriff's Office had a loose wire and did not record.

Dan died on his way to the hospital.

In Burton, it's still the talk of the town. And as always, Scott Weber's is the loudest voice.

"Here's the thing that strikes me as odd about this case," Weber says. "If you've just shot-gunned somebody through the chest, one of two things are gonna happen. You're gonna get the death penalty if they catch you or you're gonna be in prison for the rest of your life. So, you better do the witness, too. What's the difference? The penalty's the same. If you see the guy's on the floor with a gaping wound in his chest from a 12-gauge, why wouldn't you at least beat her head in with the shotgun butt?"

The Burton papers—the *MapleLeaf*, the *Geauga Times Courier*—covered the incident and moved on, but the BurtonBlog posted updates on the investigation almost daily. From the beginning, Weber has challenged Ricker's story.

In a post from June 1, titled: *Murder! The Murderer! Get him . . .* , Weber wrote: "Deceased gets tied up by a guy with a long shotgun in his hands? Pretty hard to do, try it sometime. . . . The logistics of this murder as given by the girl just don't stick to the wall."

Adding to the air of doubt and mystery is the fact that Maryann has not spoken publicly, to defend herself or to demand justice for Dan.

"If my girlfriend just got killed by a home invader, I'd be out there addressing civic groups, law enforcement groups, hiring a private investigator, talking to the media, etc," Weber wrote in a June 15 update. The only response to Weber's comments from the Ricker family was this e-mail from Maryann's 12-year-old niece, which Weber posted on June 24: "Ok, 1st of all, my Aunt Mary didn't kill ANYONE! So stop blaming her for it?! They are both honest and loving people."

Maryann's only public statement even related to the murder was made in an ad she placed in a weekly shopper a couple of months later: "Thank you . . . to all my family and friends for all your support, gifts, and flowers, after the tragic, unexpected death of my boyfriend, Dan Ott. A special thanks to all my clients at Hair Plus for their understanding and patience during my time of leave. Thank you to Brad Hess and all the girls for taking over my responsibilities during my absence. I'll be back soon!"

> **"You're gonna get the death penalty if they catch you. So you better do the witness."**

Many found the public notice troubling. Advertising your return to work doesn't seem logical if you're the only witness to a murder and you believe the killer is still on the loose.

Weber reported that agents from the Bureau of Criminal Investigation and Identification had collected evidence, including fingerprints, from the crime scene, to be processed at their lab in Richfield. He learned from the sheriff that cigarette butts had been found outside the house and that a seven-man team from the Sheriff's Department is working the case, interviewing people while waiting for results from the crime lab.

Weber is also intrigued by the fact no shell casing was found in the house. Without the casing, it's impossible to say for certain which weapon killed Dan. Most shotguns automatically discharge the spent shell. "Either he had a closed-breach gun, like one of these here, where the shell doesn't come out," says Weber, pointing to a gun on a shelf behind him, "or he shot it and didn't pump it. Or he picked it up on the way out."

As he continues reviewing the case in the back of the Gunrunner, Weber concedes there may be another explanation for the murder. "I've dated about four hairstylists," he says. "They've all got stalkers and they've all got these satellite dudes that are hanging around them. Because think about it: you get a real lonely-heart guy, he comes in there and gets his hair cut, what's the girl doing? *Touching* him. That girl's friggin' rubbing against him. She's listening to him like a shrink. They can form this really weird union, like I told [Sheriff Dan] McClelland, if there was a shooter and it wasn't Ricker, he's in that appointment book at the hair salon."

In the months following Dan's murder, Sheriff McClelland has been featured in several national TV interviews, but not to talk about the unsolved case. He's on TV to talk about his pet Chihuahua, Midge, which he has trained as a drug sniffing K-9.

The occasional media request for updates on the investigation are forwarded to Lt. John Hiscox, the public information officer for the Geauga County Sheriff's Office. "You should write about Baby Doe" instead, he suggests. "Back in the mid-'90s, a mailman discovered the body of a newborn in a ditch. It had been dismembered by animals. We'd like to know who did it."

He offered an exclusive interview with the retired detective working the Baby Doe case. Then he ushered me out of the room.

On the other side of Dan's old house, about 500 feet from the front door, is the homestead of a young Amish woman. There's a buggy parked out back. She arrives at the door flanked by two children. The woman wears a simple blue dress and has wispy salt-and-pepper hair. Her son has recently cried, his eyes red and puffy. Her daughter is about four years old, blond. She sucks her thumb quietly as the woman tells what she knows.

"I was up at 5:30 A.M.," she says. "I didn't leave the house. I didn't hear anything. No gunshot. I didn't see anything."

Across the street, Ken Sinkenbring is setting up for a family reunion. He's a kind man with a firm handshake and today he's wearing a Budweiser t-shirt and a Budweiser baseball cap while drinking

The scene of the crime. No one heard the gunshot.

a Budweiser. Standing next to him, his brother-in-law silently mocks him in a Guinness t-shirt and matching cap.

"I got up about 6 A.M.," says Sinkenbring. "I didn't hear anything. I knew Dan. He didn't do drugs, didn't drink, wasn't in debt." When he talks about the time Dan helped him wrangle up a cow that had gotten loose from his farm and wandered into Urban Growers territory, his wife stops him short. It's not good to let other farmers know that they lost a cow.

"Thing is, we don't have many neighbors out here, as you can see," says Sinkenbring, gesturing to the expanse of forest in the valley behind Dan's house that seems to stretch to Canada. "If it's a random killing, that's a scary thought. If it's not random, what does that mean?"

John Urbanowicz is working across the street at his greenhouse. He was Dan's boss and friend. His aunt owned the house where Dan was living. He says there was no sign of a shotgun blast in the house or trauma of any kind, but some carpet was missing.

· · ·

That night, my phone rings. It's a guy named Brad Hess. "Maryann wants to talk," he says. Hess is Ricker's manager at the Hair Plus salon in Middletown, five miles east of Burton. "But she thinks you're working with Weber. He's the one that needs to be shut up.'"

Seems Weber has already blogged about our interview, and this, apparently, is the basis of Hess's claim that the gunrunner and I are in cahoots. He cannot be dissuaded from this, even when informed that Ricker did not respond to efforts to reach her before Weber's blog post.

> *"It just didn't seem like she was as upset as she should have been at the funeral."*

Ricker's relatives are not helpful, either. A man who confirms he is a "close relation" says Ricker doesn't want to speak to any media but agrees to pass along the request.

Later, a friend of Maryann's, Mary Jo Newport, calls to speak on her behalf. "The police have not told her what to do," says Newport. "However, they have made strong recommendations that it would hurt the case if Maryann was verbal about the case. If there was a case, it could hurt it. Everyone who knows Maryann, knows her as a loving and caring person. And honest. People love gossip. They love to criticize. I don't know what they should expect. What do people expect? Should she go off and kill herself in her bedroom? Is she not allowed to exist now?

"The police are still investigating. They don't have the evidence back yet. Why is it taking so long? We need to get this killer off the streets.

"The only thing I wanted to let you know is that [Weber] twists and turns things. He's kind of like the Howard Stern of Burton. He'll say anything to get publicity, say anything to get attention."

But Scott Weber isn't the only one beginning to question Ricker's sincerity.

"It just didn't seem like she was as upset as she should have been at the funeral," says Frank Workman, who had known Dan since middle school. "I saw her laughing at the viewing. She was there with a guy. I didn't know who he was, if it was a brother or what. But she was laughing." It's possible the man was Maryann's boss from

Burton, a bucolic village in Geauga County, is known for its maple syrup—hence the nickname "Pancaketown."

the hair salon, as some have suggested, there to console his friend, but neither he nor Maryann would verify this.

Workman stayed in touch with Dan on an almost weekly basis until his friend's death. They talked about everything—except Maryann. Dan never mentioned her to Workman until Dan's sister broached the subject at Christmas. "Oh, it's nothing serious," Dan said at the time.

There were undercover detectives at the viewing and funeral, says Workman. They were keeping a watchful eye on guests and writing down license plates in the parking lot.

Ken Kishman was also rankled by the presence of the man at Maryann's side during the funeral. "Who the fuck is *that* guy?" he recalls thinking. "Who's going to bring some guy to her boyfriend's funeral?"

Also puzzling is what Maryann said to the congregation at St. Mary's Church in Vermilion, that morning. According to Workman and Kishman, who were present, Dan's father asked Maryann loudly to tell everyone what Dan had said to her before he died.

"He said, 'I'm sorry, Maryann, I thought that man was going to rape you.'"

"That doesn't make sense," says Kishman. He doesn't believe it would be possible for Dan to have said anything after taking a shotgun blast to the chest. "Being an avid hunter, I know what kind of damage a shotgun can do. No way are you going to get all that out."

If he were in Maryann's position, he'd be on the phone to *America's Most Wanted*. "I think it's selfish of her not to go on the record. She has so far done nothing to help find Dan's killer. Her doing nothing is not going to help. She needs to get off her ass and do something."

A source who asked to remain anonymous suggested to me that the full picture of what took place in Dan's living room the morning of May 26 is yet to be revealed. This person claimed to have direct knowledge that Maryann told police the masked intruder had approached Dan and asked what his name was before he shot him and that the shooting had occurred outside, on the front steps, which supports Urbanowicz's theory that no gun was discharged inside the small house.

"That is one of the statements that Maryann has told us," says Sheriff McClelland when reached by phone. McClelland also confirms that Maryann was sequestered without a lawyer for several hours after the shooting and was subjected to a voice stress test, a type of lie detector.

When asked if he could share the results of that test, McClelland says, "I cannot."

When asked if Maryann is considered a suspect in Dan Ott's murder, McClelland says, "We have a number of people we have not ruled out. The investigation has yet to focus on a specific person. We continue to work on it very diligently. It's not a simple case."

Another person detectives are interested in is a troubled young man named Ryan Yost, who once lived in the house where Dan was killed. Yost had several run-ins with the Geauga County Sheriff's officers while he was still a juvenile. After his family moved to another section of town, Yost worked with Dan at Urban Growers. According to friends of Maryann, Yost called Dan shortly before the murder and they argued on the phone about a job.

Sheriff McClelland, however, seems decidedly unimpressed with Yost as a suspect. "Our detectives are aware of this individual and have followed up on that information," he says in a tired voice.

Gail Yost, Ryan's mother, says detectives have been to her house but have not questioned her son, who was with his father the day Dan was murdered. She explains that the phone call her son made to Dan was to ask about another job at Urban Growers to fulfill a school-to-work program requirement.

"Ryan looked up to Dan," she says. "Once, when he was working with Dan at Urban Growers, Ryan dropped an expensive piece of equipment and Dan paid for it so that Ryan wouldn't get into trouble with the owner. Dan was the nicest guy."

In Pancaketown, the scuttlebutt continues.

Anyone with information related to this crime should contact detectives at 440-279-2009.

CHAPTER 10

Hiding in Plain Sight

The Unsolved Suicide of Joseph Newton Chandler

Sherman, Texas: December 21, 1945

Our mystery begins with a tragic confluence of events that occurred along a dark stretch of country road just before Christmas, not long after the end of the second World War.

The Chandler family are in their 1941 sedan, driving south through Sherman, on their way to Grandma's house in Weatherford. The Chandlers live in Tulsa, Oklahoma, where Joe Chandler II is a field rep for Buick Motor Company. His wife, Billie, and their only child, eight-year-old Joe the Third, are with him in the car, packed between wrapped presents and luggage. They are planning to spend the holidays in Texas.

There is a man driving a car headed north, a ways down the road. He doesn't know the Chandlers. And that's a blessing, really. Considering what happens next.

In the road between them, a truck full of lumber has pulled to the side of the northbound lane, resting halfway on the shoulder. Probability is on the man's side—this is not a busy highway. Chances are, there won't be any cars coming the other way, not for those few seconds it will take to correct himself if he swerves to avoid it.

It's like hitting the lottery, then, when he does hit the Chandler sedan as it approaches from the other direction. The vehicles collide head-on. The man survives. The Chandlers do not. The presents in the car are donated to a local charity; the bodies are laid to rest near Grandma's house.

Eastlake, Ohio: July 30, 2002

Judging by the position of the body, it appeared the old man was looking at his reflection in the mirror when he put the gun in his mouth and blew out the left side of his skull.

Detective Christopher Bowersock found him lying in a sticky pool of coagulated blood inside the cramped bathroom of the efficiency that was rented out to Joseph Newton Chandler. The stink was so bad—this was the one of the hottest days of a very hot summer—that Detective Bowersock was forced back outside, where he waited until someone could bring air packs from the station. Neighbors had noticed a smell coming from apartment D and had altered a Dover Apartments manager, who called the police. But, inside, it was much worse.

The detective got a better look at the efficiency when he went in again, this time breathing through an air filter. It was a single room, divided in a corner by a waist-high wooden bar. On one side was the kitchenette—toaster oven, mini fridge, tiny stovetop. On the other was the living room/bedroom. A Murphy bed, covered in a patterned flannel sheet was in the "down" position. Across from this was a couch sitting below a framed picture of a castle in Spain—both of which probably came with the furnished efficiency. A TV was set against the window in the front wall. Next to the bed was an open closet. Inside the closet was a pair of work pants and a plain button-up shirt, looking lonely next to two clip-on ties hanging beside them, and a tweed hat. Sitting on the wooden bar was an antiquated computer, two books (*How to Make Money in Stocks* and *Making Money with Your Computer at Home*), and an open gun case, the kind with gray pointy foam inside.

The bathroom was covered in '70s-era yellow wallpaper, which was mostly obscured by a legion of flies scuttling across it. They buzzed and dived around the detective as he bent to the body, which had fallen, face down, in the corner in front of the mirror, about a

The man who called himself Joseph Newton Chandler rented a one-room efficiency in this Eastlake apartment complex.

week before. Detective Bowersock pulled an arm to move the body and felt it slide from the torso like "a drumstick being pulled from a well-cooked chicken." Maggots poured out of the hole in the head and landed on the floor.

Under the body was the handgun, a five-shot revolver, with four live rounds still in the spinner. It was an old gun. Much older than the case that was lying on the counter.

The police double-bagged the body for the coroner.

To Detective Bowersock, it seemed like a simple suicide.

He was about to learn that nothing about this case was as simple as it seemed.

The emergency contact listed on Joe Chandler's rental application was a man named Mike, Joe's one and only friend, if he could even be called that. Mike asked me not to publish his last name, because he's tired of the notoriety that has come with being the Mystery Man's executor.

Mike hadn't seen Joe in at least four months when he found out he was dead. He and his wife were on vacation when it happened.

When they returned, there were several messages waiting on the answering machine, from the police and the coroner's office. They wanted him to ID the body.

Mike had met Joe while working at Lubrizol, an east side chemical plant. Joe was a talented electrical engineer, employed by a temp company called Comprehensive Designers, Inc., even though he had basically worked full time at Lubrizol for 12 years, beginning in 1986. He designed new equipment, handling everything from drawing to scheduling installers. And he fixed anything that needed fixing in the plant. For this, he was paid $17 an hour, earning $36,000 a year. Mike's office was located right next to Joe's, so he got to know him about as well as anyone could.

> **Mike noticed that whenever someone asked how old he was, Joe always gave a different age.**

Joe Chandler was quite peculiar. He wore factory-style protective eyeglasses, even outside of work. He stood about five foot eight and looked to be in his 60s, although Mike noticed that whenever someone asked how old he was, Joe always gave a different age. He had larger-than-average hands, with thick, not extremely long, fingers. He smelled like he didn't bathe often. And he was always making little gadgets.

Joe built himself a white-noise machine that piped static through headphones which he wore at all times. He kept it turned up so loud you could hear it if you were standing close to him. Joe also wired his TV to shut off during commercial breaks and click back on when the program started up again—he hated advertisements of all kinds. As a favor to another co-worker named Mark Herendeen, Joe once rigged the Madison Fire Department's alarm system so that it turned on the lights in the sleeping area whenever it sounded.

Joe also had a habit of disappearing. Occasionally, he would call Mike and explain he wouldn't be coming to work for a while. "They're getting close," Joe would say. Usually, he was only gone for a few days, although at least once he was gone for months.

"I should have suspected something," says Mike, thinking back. "But I didn't. I just thought he was a paranoid schizophrenic or something."

Private Investigator Mike Lewis tracked down the real Joseph Newton Chandler's family.

Mike felt sorry for Joe; he didn't seem to have *anyone*. He never mentioned family. He carried around a notepad with lists of restaurants that were open for Thanksgiving and Christmas, for Christ's sake. So, he invited Joe to have supper at his apartment one evening. The meal was awkward. Joe wasn't much of a conversationalist. But eventually, he gave up a few more details. He told Mike he had once been married to a Cuban woman and had lived in Florida.

When Mike's wife, Marilyn, celebrated her 50th birthday with a costume party, they invited Joe, both thinking that he would never show up, "not in a million years." To everyone's surprise, Joe showed up dressed head-to-toe as a mobster—pinstripe suit, fedora, cigar.

After Joe was laid off from Lubrizol in 1997, Mike made a point to call him at least once a year. During one such call, he noticed that Joe sounded frail. So, Mike drove out to Joe's efficiency on Lakeshore Boulevard, a converted Knights Inn hotel room.

Joe *was* frail. He had just had surgery. He told Mike that he had rectal cancer and the prognosis was not good.

"His doctor wanted to give him chemo," says Mike. "But he couldn't afford it." Joe insisted on paying for everything in cash and

172 | THE SERIAL KILLER'S APPRENTICE

his surgery had set him back about $80,000. Mike tried to get him on Medicare or some other plan, but Joe refused.

"He could hardly hear me," says Mike. "His eyes were bad, too." In fact, Joe needed help filling out his new lease. "That's when I got myself in trouble."

Mike saw that Joe had listed an apartment manager as his emergency contact. So, he offered to put his own name there, instead. "My God, that was the beginning of it. That's how I got dragged into this."

Because his name was listed on the lease, and because the courts couldn't find anyone better, Mike became executor of Joe's estate. It became his responsibility to track down Joe's next-of-kin so that his assets could be distributed. Assets that included those clip on ties, the out-of-date computer, and the $82,000 in cash and stocks Joe had left in his bank account.

Mike didn't know where to begin. His wife worked for an attorney in town, though, so Mike went to him for help. The attorney recommended they hire a private eye. And he already had one in mind.

As chief investigator at Confidential Investigative Services, it takes a lot to surprise Mike Lewis. He's seen it all—workers' comp winners cheating the system, politicians sneaking out on their wives, sports stars sneaking out on their mistresses, media magnates consorting with young women in the Metroparks. Cheating is his bread and butter. And Joe Chandler was, in the end, a cheater, too. Lewis would soon realize that Joe had cheated the government out of an identity.

"I thought it was a fairly simple case, at first," says Lewis. "Then, I did the normal database search and there was nothing on this guy."

No criminal record, no military service record, no credit history.

On his 401K application, Lewis discovered Joe had listed the name of a sister and a brother as beneficiaries: a Mary R. Wilson, of Columbus, and a George Chandler, in Denver, Colorado. But under "telephone," Joe had written "none," and when Lewis ran the addresses, he found they were fictitious.

Lewis tried his luck with Joe's birth certificate. A certified copy of the certificate was issued to Joe on August 29, 1978. It had been sent from Buffalo, New York, where Joe was born. The certificate stated that Joe's father was born in Weatherford, Texas. Maybe he could find a surviving relative still living near there.

Bingo.

In Fort Worth, he found Dan Chandler, a distant relative who acted strangely when Lewis told him Joe Chandler was dead. After that initial conversation, Lewis could not get Dan back on the phone. He quickly learned Dan had hired his own investigator. That PI eventually found a newspaper clipping detailing the accident that killed Joe Chandler and his parents in Sherman, Texas, in 1945. The man in Eastlake was an imposter.

Bound by limited resources provided by "Joe's" estate, Lewis could not afford to do much more leg work. But he did find one more important clue: Joe had apparently used the copy of his birth certificate to get a social security card under that name, as well. He had applied for a card on September, 25, 1978. The card was mailed to an address in South Dakota. The signature on the social security card application matched the signature on the lease for the Eastlake efficiency.

"This guy was real thorough," says Lewis. "He used the same fake address for his sister for 10 years. He had a system down."

Now that Joe Chandler was officially a John Doe, the Eastlake police got interested again. Detectives retrieved Joe's possessions from Mike and combed through the stuff looking for some evidence that could point them to the man's true identity. Who had been hiding in their town for almost 20 years?

Joe had a key ring with seven keys on it when he died. One was for his truck, a 1988 GMC pickup, which he had paid for with cash. Another was for his safe, which contained financial documents that yielded nothing new. The purpose of the other five was anyone's guess.

Detectives sent various items to the crime lab to be dusted for

Left: The only known photograph of the mysterious "Joseph Newton Chandler", from his driver's license. Right: A composite sketch of the Zodiac killer—what "Chandler" might have looked like when he was younger? *(Eastlake Police Department)*

fingerprints, including an ashtray they discovered in the pickup (Joe didn't smoke). When they got the results back, they fed the information into several databases. They got two hits. One for Mike Lewis, the private eye, who had handled the documents at some point, and one for an Eastlake detective who had processed the crime scene.

They got lucky when they ran down the gun's serial number. It had been sold in 1966, in Seagoville, Texas, a town less than 80 miles from Weatherford.

The police also got a copy of Joe's social security year-by-year earnings statement. His income was listed annually from 1978 to 2002. It was interrupted, strangely, in 1983, when there had been no reported income.

They tried to fire up Joe's computer, to see if he'd left any files on the hard drive, but it had been damaged in the move from the efficiency. No one could get it running, so they threw it away.

On a job application, detectives learned Joe claimed to have been employed by a company called Wilson & Associates in Los Angeles, California, from 1975 to 1980. When reached, a Wilson & Associates manager said he had no such record.

The Rapid City lead was run down, too. Joe's social security card had been sent to 2326½ Canyon Lake Drive. Sergeant Tom Senesac, of the Rapid City Police Department, offered to check out the address. It was a slum, little more than a shack, tucked behind a ramshackle house. The home's owner was long dead and the man's son could not remember who had rented the place in 1978.

"We don't even know if he actually lived there, or if he was just checking the mailbox periodically," says Sergeant Senesac. He checked the crisscross directory at the local library to see who was listed under that address. He found the name of a local pothead listed in 1977 and 1979, but no one under 1978. The pothead has been accounted for. He's dead, too.

"He had to have a cool secret, whoever he was," says Senesac. "I started thinking about what was happening in history back then. This wasn't too long after D.B. Cooper hijacked that airplane and got away with $200,000, you know? I teased my buddy at the FBI about that for a while. But he swears D.B. died when he jumped out of the plane."

Soon, the leads dried up and the detectives moved on to more important matters. After all, there was really no evidence of a crime, here.

Eager to pick up where the police left off, web sleuths were about to turn Joe Chandler into a legend.

2008

Typing "Joseph Newton Chandler" into Google calls up several amateur detective websites, each with increasingly outlandish theories for who Joe Chandler really was. Everyone from D.B. Cooper to Jim Morrison (no kidding) is suspected. By sheer volume, the leading contender is currently the Zodiac Killer.

Zodiac was a serial killer who once haunted northern California. He dispatched five victims (mostly couples, as they parked in lovers' lanes or picnicked in a park) between December 1968 and October 1969. He sent taunting messages to the police and newspaper reporters, daring them to catch him. But no one ever did. The case remains unsolved. To this day, no one knows why Zodiac stopped killing and vanished in 1969. Some suspect he moved away from California, after the police got close, and perhaps quietly continued his spree elsewhere.

When the story of Joe Chandler's suicide hit the web, Zodiac buffs noticed a similarity between a drawing that someone had done of what Joe might have looked like in his 30s and the composite sketch of Zodiac. They noted that Joe had some ties to California and that there had been a rash of murders that mirrored the Zodiac crimes in Ohio between 1979 and 1982. Known as the Ohio Lovers Murders, eight couples were killed while parked in secluded necking spots from Toledo to Akron.

In his letters to police, Zodiac had often made allusions to Jack the Ripper. Blogger Steve Huff, who has studied both Zodiac and Jack the Ripper, recognized Joe Chandler's name immediately. A London investigator named Joseph Chandler found one of Jack the Ripper's victims. If Zodiac had wanted a new identity, Joe Chandler was perfect.

"That's a tangential link, easily dismissed as coincidence," writes Huff at Huff's Crime Blog. "Still, hair stood up on the back of my neck when I saw it."

Another researcher named Mike Rodelli stumbled upon a death certificate for another Joseph Chandler who died in San Rafael, California, just north of Zodiac's stomping grounds, in 1994. That Joseph Chandler died on July 24, eight years to the day before Joe Chandler committed suicide in Eastlake, according to the Lake County coroner's best estimate, based on the condition of the body.

But there is no hard evidence to link Joe Chandler to the Zodiac. And a much more compelling explanation for who Joe might have been was recently put forth by a computer technician—and part-time blogger—from Oklahoma named Chris Yarbrough.

Yarbrough runs Crimeshadows.com, a website devoted to the Zodiac as well as other unsolved murders throughout the United States. He has an odd hobby—in his spare time, Yarbrough likes to pore through old mug shots on city websites. He is specifically interested in any fugitives from the late '70s, early '80s. He's looking for the Zodiac, of course, believing it's possible the killer was arrested somewhere as he fled California. In January 2006, he stumbled upon the mug shot of Stephen Craig Campbell, who skipped town after being arrested for attempted murder in Cheyenne, Wyo-

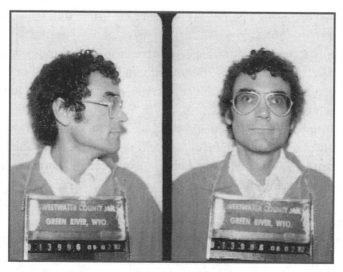

Stephen Craig Campbell, who looked a lot like Chandler, has eluded authorities for decades. *(Sweetwater County Sheriff's Department)*

ming, in 1982. He noticed that Stephen Campbell looked a lot like Joe Chandler.

And the more he looked, the more connections he uncovered between Campbell and the man who committed suicide in Eastlake.

"A lot of things click," says Yarbrough. "There are some discrepancies, too, but nothing that cannot be explained."

Cheyenne, Wyoming 1982

Stephen Craig Campbell was, by all accounts, a brilliant electrical engineer. He was born in California, grew up near Houston, Texas, and received a mechanical engineering degree from the University of Arkansas. He worked for Stoffer Chemicals in 1982, at their trona mine. He wore large, thick, corrective lenses, even when he wasn't at work. He had bigger than average hands. Co-workers described him as a loner, interested in ham radio, photography, and chess. He kept a small plane at the local airport, which he flew occasionally. And when he found out his wife was having an affair, he tinkered with a homemade gadget—a small bomb that he packed into a toolbox and left on his back porch for the other man to find during his next visit.

Only, Campbell hadn't expected his wife to find the toolbox first. Sensing something amiss, she got a broom and nudged the box with the handle. The bomb exploded, blowing off the back of the house and a portion of her hand.

Campbell was arrested and charged with attempted murder in Sweetwater County. He made bail and disappeared. The Sheriff's Department and Bureau of Alcohol, Tobacco, and Firearms agents have been trying to find him ever since.

"He had a number of aliases and social security numbers we suspected he was using," says Sweetwater County Sheriff's Lieutenant Detective Burke Morin. "Obviously, we never found him. But we thought we were close a couple times."

Campbell is suspected of undergoing minor plastic surgery to alter his appearance, funded, perhaps, by a rich uncle.

Their best lead came from an acquaintance of Campbell's who, in an odd twist of fate, bumped into him while vacationing in the Virgin Islands in the '80s. By the time ATF got there, Campbell was gone.

For a while, Campbell was also a top suspect in the Unabomber case. The intricate wiring he had used in the bomb he had left on his back porch was similar to the care the Unabomber had used in his incendiary packages.

ATF Special Agent Ken Bray has pursued Campbell for a quarter of a century, at times coming close, but never quite getting his man. "He got caught using an alias, once," says Bray. "But then he switched names and disappeared again."

Campbell's sister still lives in Texas but tells detectives she has not heard from her brother for a long time.

In the summer of 2002, a Sweetwater County detective briefly reopened their investigation and started tracking back leads again, contacting those who knew Campbell. But the file was closed again in October of that year.

•   •   •

2008 Again

Chris Yarbrough lists the connections between Joe Chandler and Stephen Campbell on his website. He points out that Cheyenne, Wyoming is 300 miles from Rapid City, South Dakota, where Joe got his fake social security card in 1978.

But there are some things that don't match up. Stephen Campbell was six foot two, significantly taller than Joe, at five foot eight. Campbell had brown eyes, Joe had gray eyes, according to his driver's license. And Campbell's hair was curly, while Joe's was straight.

> *To his neighbors at Dover Apartments, Joe didn't seem dangerous. Just strange.*

"These discrepancies could be explained by the aging process," suggests Yarbrough. "People lie on the driver's licenses all the time. It wouldn't be that hard to lie about one's height." And as for the hair? "I seem to remember permanents being quite popular for men in the early '80s."

Compelling enough already, the idea becomes more intriguing after reviewing the case with Mike Lewis, the private eye who first realized Joe was not who he appeared to be. "The computer the police threw away still worked when I was on the case," he says. "I had a guy I know comb through it. He found a couple of searches Joe had made on the Internet prior to his death. One search was on Nazism. The other was a search for information on plastic explosives."

Joe's neighbors at Dover Apartments don't recall the man ever being racist. He didn't seem dangerous, either. Just strange. "I saw him walking every day," says Wayne McNutt, in apartment A. "He'd walk over to Nick's Family Restaurant and have breakfast. Even in the winter, he'd be out there walking in his work clothes. But he always looked straight ahead when he walked. Never made eye contact."

The woman who lived beside him remembers a middle-aged woman with dark hair visiting Joe's apartment, once, a short time before he died. She thought it was his daughter, but can't say for sure. Other than that instance, she never saw Joe with company.

Joe's co-worker from Lubrizol is still executor of his estate, although the account has dwindled over the years to pay for investigators and court costs. Mike would like to know who he's helping, someday. He has many questions about the case that beg answers. How did an ashtray end up in Joe's truck, if the man never smoked? Who was the man in the photograph a woman from the coroner's office showed him in 2005? He was sure it was Joe and the mystery was solved.

That man's name was Elmer Liskey, a local musician and real estate salesman, according to the Lake County coroner's office. But he was ruled out after coroner's investigators discovered that Liskey had died in 1999.

"Maybe he was just a spook," says Detective Bowersock, shrugging his shoulders. "You know, an old CIA operative who saw too much and wanted somewhere safe to live out the remainder of his life."

Whoever Joe Chandler really was, he died with his powerful secret locked away in his eccentric mind. His ashes are safely entombed at Riverside Cemetery, in a wall facing west, under a name that is not his own.

CHAPTER 11

West End Girls

The Unsolved Disappearances of
Amanda Berry and Georgina DeJesus

The cassettes came wrapped in a crumpled envelope. A short note explained that these tapes contained important information about Amanda Berry's disappearance. The letter was signed "Jack Bauer." The return address belonged to a local Burger King.

A woman's voice, midwestern, middle-aged, floated out of the tape like narration from some long-forgotten dream. "My name is Robin Dedeker," said the voice. "I'm a psychic medium. I'm doing a reading for the family of Amanda M. Berry and the date today is August 19, 2005. I am located in Minnesota."

Slowly, over the course of the next two hours, Dedeker described a vision of Amanda—or "Mandy," as her friends called her—and what happened to her the day she vanished into the smoggy air of Cleveland's west wide. This message was intended for Mandy's mother, Louwana Miller, but it never reached her ears. Instead, Louwana gave it to a young magician obsessed with finding her daughter—a man who wanted to be an FBI agent and who sometimes calls himself Jack Bauer. The magician sent it to me.

Now, Louwana is dead. And if the psychic is to be believed, Mandy is, too. And if Mandy is dead, what does that mean for Georgina DeJesus, the girl who disappeared a year later from the same beat-down stretch of Lorain Avenue where Mandy was last seen?

Many have wondered if the two disappearances are connected, if this is just the beginning of a serial killer's spree.

What happened to Mandy and Gina? Are they still alive someplace, together, kept by some deviant that detectives have yet to track down? Or have they crossed over to the other side, unable to communicate their secrets to anyone except the most gifted psychic?

"Amanda's death occurred on what would have been her 17th birthday," Dedeker's voice claims confidently, soothingly. "This location where Amanda went with these three young men is somewhat isolated. It's a park. It's near the water. I can see the city."

Barely over five feet tall, Mandy was nicknamed "Shortie." She was an attractive girl, with Native American lineage—her great-grandmother was Cherokee—evident in her high cheekbones and brown eyes.

She grew up on the side of Cleveland where the sun always sets, in a house on West 111th, so close to I-90 that commuter traffic was the ambient background music to her abbreviated life. She shut out the din of the city around her by escaping into books. She read with a ferocity that still amazes family members—books, magazines, anything she could get her hands on.

Around the time Mandy became a teenager, her father skipped town and returned to family in Tennessee, leaving behind Mandy, her mother Louwana, and an older sister named Beth. They managed the best they could. When Beth got married, she moved into the apartment downstairs with her husband, Teddy Serrano, who became the de facto patriarch of the clan. Mandy babysat Beth's children.

Mandy attended John Marshall High, a public school on West 140th that is locked up tighter than some prisons. She hated it, wanted no part in the drama of inner-city high school life. So Mandy researched home schooling. She figured out a way to take courses online and paid for books herself. She organized her schedule in a way that allowed her to finish weekly classes in three days instead

Left: Amanda "Mandy" Berry studied from home to avoid the dangers of an inner-city high school. Right: What Mandy might look like today. *(www.missingkids.com/FBI)*

of five, locking herself inside while she studied, not answering the phone until all the work was finished. At home, Mandy excelled. She would have graduated at 17.

At 16, Mandy got a job at the Burger King at the corner of West 110 and Lorain. It was a short walk from her house, but she often got a ride from friends or her mother because she didn't want to walk alone. Beth's husband, Teddy, worked there, too.

April 21, 2003, a day before her 17th birthday, Mandy was scheduled to work at Burger King until 8 P.M. Louwana and Beth worked at a nearby factory and planned to return home at about the same time. Teddy also worked at Burger King that day.

According to published accounts, Beth called Mandy on her cell phone around 7:45 P.M. Mandy told her that she had gotten off early and was going to get a ride home. She was last seen sitting at a table inside the restaurant, waiting, looking out the window.

· · ·

Nearly a year later, Mandy's "missing" poster hung in the window of that Burger King, slowly fading from white to cataract-yellow in the sunlight, as a 14-year-old girl named Georgina DeJesus walked toward a pay phone across the street.

Georgina was older than most of her class-mates at Wilbur Wright Middle School. She was in special ed classes and still learning how to read in the seventh grade. But she loved music—J-Lo and Aaliyah, mostly—and she loved to dance. She was active, always running off to slumber parties, baseball games, or to roller skate at the neighborhood rink.

> **Many have won-dered if the two disappearances are connected, if this is the begin-ning of a serial killer's spree.**

Georgina was her father's mother's middle name, a tribute to a woman who raised a large and sprawling family well known in the Hispanic community that surrounds their home on West 71st. Gina shared a special bond with her namesake. It was her grandmother who first felt that trouble was stalking Gina. Something was going to happen to the girl, she told her son. And he felt it too, like a slow-moving steamroller bearing down on his family.

Felix DeJesus was so unnerved by this feeling of doom that he spoke to his boss at the factory where he ground down saw bands and asked if he could start leaving work early so that he could pick Gina up after school. For while, he did. But eventually, his boss grew impatient and asked him to switch back to full workdays. On Friday, April 2, 2004, Felix gave Gina money to take an RTA bus home and hoped that the feeling in his stomach was only a concerned father's paranoia.

That day, Gina wore a tan shirt, black bellbottom hip-huggers, and a white sweater. On her feet were white and blue Phat Farm specials. In her pockets was $1.25 for bus fare. But Gina didn't take the bus. Instead, she gave 50 cents to a friend to make a phone call. The friend wanted to go to Gina's for the evening. They could have walked the long stretch of Lorain to Gina's house together.

Gina's friend used the pay phone at Lorain and West 105 at around 2:30 P.M. The friend's mother said the girl had to come home,

Left: Georgina "Gina" DeJesus would never have accepted a ride from a stranger. Right: What Gina might look like today. *(FBI)*

though, so after the call, they went their separate ways, alone. Gina was last seen walking east on Lorain.

Mandy and Gina's whereabouts remain unknown. Gina's posters have joined Mandy's in the abandoned storefront windows of Lorain Avenue. And while the public waits for news and hopes for closure, FBI agents and Cleveland detectives continue to investigate leads until they dead-end.

Mandy's mother, Louwana Miller, died March 2, 2006. Doctors said it was heart failure. Her daughter Beth said she died of a broken heart, caused by Mandy's disappearance and exacerbated by a recent visit to the *Montel Williams* show where a psychic told her that Mandy had been murdered.

Both girls' names appeared in the news again in September 2006 when police and FBI raided a home on West 50th and held the owner and a tenant in jail under suspicion of murdering Gina. They got a

Gina's route (lighter dotted line)

1. Wilbur Wright Middle School
2. Gina's friend uses pay phone here
3. Bloodhounds lose Gina's scent here

Amanda's route (darker dotted line)

4. Burger King
5. Her home; also her last known whereabouts

A map of the area where Mandy and Gina disappeared. Is it coincidence that they vanished so close to each other? Or is this section of town the hunting ground of one man? *(Ron Kretsch)*

tip that owner Matthew Hurayt had buried the girl under concrete in his garage. Hundreds of people gathered around the house, lured by news helicopters that hovered over the house for hours. Word on the street was that Mandy was buried there, too.

Hurayt seemed like a good suspect. He was a registered sex predator with a history of assault, convicted in 1987 for forcing a boy to have sex.

A pair of women's white shoes was found in his attic. But they were not Gina's. And there were no bodies under the garage, so police eventually let the men go. Hurayt's lawyer proclaimed his innocence, but vigilantes dealt their own dose of justice to the man with the shady past living in their midst. He still owned the house on West 50th a year later, but, by then, each window had been broken and video cameras were mounted around the perimeter.

·   ·   ·

In early 2007, members of Mandy and Gina's families met with me inside FBI headquarters on Lakeside Avenue. Gina's parents, Nancy Ruiz and Felix DeJesus, sat on one side of a large conference table. Mandy's sister, Beth, and aunt, Theresa Miller, sat on the other. Also present was FBI spokesman Scott Wilson and a victims' liaison.

Rarely does the FBI grant access to those involved in open investigations. The hope was that this story might spark new leads. The agents and detectives still searching for the girls want these cases solved as much as the families do. But as the conversation progressed, Wilson made sure certain information was kept secret, especially information involving uncharged suspects. And for good reason, after the incident with Hurayt.

Beth was the first one to talk. She's tiny, like her sister; her body was nearly engulfed by the office chair in which she sat. But she was also confident. Since the death of their mother, she had assumed the role of family spokesperson.

"Mandy loved Eminem," Beth said, smiling. "She had seen his movie. She had a crush on him, thought he was cute.

"She started working at Burger King about a month or two after her 16th birthday, so she was there almost a year. She liked it. She got along with everyone."

According to Beth, six months before her sister disappeared, Mandy began dating a young man named D.J. Diaz, a handsome, light-skinned African American teen with a cool smile. But he never came around the house, and Louwana thought he was disrespectful. Sometimes, he and his friends would give Mandy a ride after work.

The last time Beth spoke to her sister was about 7:45 P.M. on the day she went missing. Mandy told her, "I'm going to get a ride. I'll call you when I get home."

"We got home about 8 P.M. and she wasn't home," said Beth. "A little after eight, we called her again. No answer. She always answered her phone. But we weren't sure something was wrong until 11:13 P.M."

"Louwana knew something was wrong when Mandy didn't

come home by 11," said Theresa, the aunt. "That was her curfew. And Mandy would always call if she was going to be late."

They left messages on Mandy's cell phone until it was full. They called the police. The next day, they made flyers and passed them out along Lorain. Louwana stayed up for three nights straight, said Theresa.

The police asked if Mandy could have run away, but Louwana showed them the money Mandy had left behind—money for a manicure and styling for her birthday party. Then, about a week and a half after Mandy disappeared, someone called Louwana from Mandy's cell phone.

"The first time he called he just hung up," said Beth. "We were watching TV and a report had just come on about Mandy. And then he called back and I picked up the other phone when my mom answered it. He sounded older. And he said, 'Your daughter is with me. And we're married. She'll be coming home in a couple days.'"

FBI spokesman Wilson confirmed that the call did indeed originate from Mandy's cell phone. The man has never called back.

"We checked in with her boyfriend to see if he saw her," said Theresa. "They always talked on the phone. But he said he hadn't heard from her."

"This has to be someone who knew her," Beth said, emotion welling up inside her slight frame. "I believe it was someone she knew well."

Across the table, Felix DeJesus sat quietly next to Nancy Ruiz. He's a large, imposing man. Stoic, but thinking. He listened to Mandy's story but he'd heard it all before. He thought about his own daughter.

Gina's parents weren't married, but they'd lived together for 28 years. They had two other children and a vast army of relatives and friends who kept them going.

"It was someone she knew," said Felix. "Gina would never have taken a ride from a stranger. Never. Not even from my own brothers. Not from my own friends. We raised up our kids like that, never to approach nobody. We taught them to run away."

By 4 P.M. on April 2, 2004, Nancy was on the phone, calling Gina's friends' parents, trying to find out why her daughter wasn't home and why she hadn't called. "I was crying, they were laughing," said Nancy. "They didn't think she could really be missing. But I told everyone I talked to to call 10 other people to look for Gina. We called police at 5:30."

When he got home and found Nancy hysterical, Felix knew his intuition had been right, that trouble had caught up with his daughter. "I started driving up and down streets," he said. "My mind was just gone. And then anger set in. I didn't know what to do. Didn't know what to do. I felt it coming. And it just kept eating at me."

> "Once something like this happens, you're suspicious of everybody."

"We were supposed to go to the mall that night. Just her and I," said Nancy, drifting someplace in her memory. "It had to be someone close to the family. She was spending a lot of time sleeping over at friends' houses and it started to make me feel uncomfortable. But once something like this happens, you're suspicious of everybody. Everyone's a suspect."

Investigators used bloodhounds to track Gina's scent from the pay phone. The dogs didn't go far. "They stopped at Lorain and 104," said Nancy. Gina's scent ended just before McKenna's Tavern, near an alley that leads back to a garbage bin and a set of steps to upstairs apartments. The dogs did go across the street, then, but Nancy believes it was just so the animals could find a proper place to urinate.

"My life has totally changed," said Felix. "Every time I sit on my porch, I find myself looking at license plates on vehicles that go by. I look at the drivers and remember what they look like. Could that person have done it? I don't look at people the same."

Wayne Gonce is an amateur magician from Maryland, a pale kid with wide, troubled eyes and a vast imagination. A fan of horror movies and sci-fi conventions and the TV show 24, he calls himself Jack Bauer, and he'd like to be the hero in this story, the one who finds Mandy.

After a fight with his father in early April 2003, Gonce moved from Maryland to his uncle's place in Newburgh Heights. He got a job at Burger King in Parma. Not long after he settled in, Mandy went missing, and Gonce became transfixed with her story. He always wanted to be an FBI agent, and this seemed like the perfect opportunity to hone his detective skills.

He attended a vigil for Mandy at the Burger King on Lorain and that's where he introduced himself to Louwana and Beth. "Is there anything I can do to help?" he asked.

Louwana told him about D.J., Mandy's boyfriend. Gonce talked to Mandy's friends and co-workers, sometimes introducing himself as an investigator who was working the case, assisting the FBI. He learned that D.J. was also dating a girl named Flannery while seeing Mandy and that Flannery was going to confront Mandy the day she disappeared.

The FBI, however, seemed more interested in Gonce himself than in the information he provided. Gonce received a call at work from Special Agent Tim Kolonik who wanted to know why he was so interested in the case. "He interrogated me and all that," says Gonce. "I told him I was interested in joining the FBI in a couple years. I helped him a little bit after that. But he doesn't call me back anymore."

When Gina went missing a year later, Gonce contacted the DeJesus family and spent his free time tracking down "leads" in that case as well. He still calls Gina's family regularly.

After Gonce sent the psychic's reading to me, it became apparent that he had a slippery view of social mores. For instance, he didn't bother getting permission from the psychic first. When Robin Dedeker learned that he'd sent tapes meant for Louwana to a reporter, using an alias and fake return address, she was angry. And then there's the strange urge that Gonce has to play "bad cop."

"I've always wanted to talk to D.J. and Flannery," he says. "I want to get them in separate rooms and play them off each other. Give one immunity, you know? And tell the other one that their partner has admitted everything. If they can do that for terrorists, they can do that for a missing girl, right?"

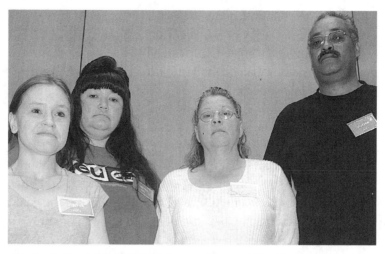

The family they left behind: Beth Serrano, Theresa Miller, Nancy Ruiz, and Felix DeJesus.

Gonce has since returned to Maryland and signed up to join the Marines. He maintains a MySpace page devoted to Mandy. The FBI did follow up on his leads, even if they eventually cut off contact with Gonce. D.J. was questioned. So was Flannery.

When I caught up with D.J. in 2006, he was washing his turquoise SUV. "I can't talk about Amanda," he said, smiling. "You can believe what you want, but I'm not gonna say anything about that."

Flannery used to live down the street from D.J. but had since moved out of her father's house. He still lived there, though, and was walking his dog while D.J. washed the SUV. "I asked my daughter about D.J. and if she knew anything about what happened to Amanda," he said. "I knew she was dating him at the same time but I never met him. She was vague about it when she answered me. But she said she didn't think D.J. was involved."

Co-workers at Burger King say Mandy had just found out that Teddy, her sister's husband, was having an affair (Teddy and Beth have since separated and Teddy has moved out of state). Mandy told co-workers the affair had made her sick to her stomach and she wanted to leave before the shift was over. On top of all this, someone called her with bad news.

"The day she left work early, she got a call here and she was crying," says Latarra Gary, who worked with her in 2003.

A law enforcement official who worked on the case, and spoke to me on the condition of anonymity, confirmed Teddy's affair and revealed more interesting information, never released to the public.

The most shocking revelation is that Mandy didn't disappear from Burger King. She made it home first.

Mandy must have changed out of her uniform, the official says, because each uniform she owned was accounted for. One uniform, possibly the one she wore that day, was found balled up and stuck behind her dresser. No one is sure if she was alone, but she could not have been there long, because Beth and Louwana returned a little after 8 P.M.

D.J. told detectives that he was at a friend's house at the time Mandy disappeared. His buddies backed him up and passed polygraph tests. Flannery, the official said, did not have an alibi but is not considered a serious suspect.

And that cell phone call, the one Louwana received from her daughter's phone a week and a half after she went missing? Investigators triangulated the signal and found it had originated somewhere near West 58th and Clark.

Persons of interest in Gina's disappearance have also been easy to find, though none has been charged with her abduction.

Across the street from where bloodhounds lost Gina's scent is a little coffee shop owned by Rich Giachetti, a boisterous Italian who inherited the property from his father. On the last day of un-enforced public smoking, I found him chaining cigarettes inside his java joint. Most of his clientele are in recovery. He doesn't want to begrudge them their last vice, but he is hanging signs alerting them of the new law so he doesn't get fined. "I don't know what it's going to do to my business," he says.

When asked about Gina, he nods and says, "The FBI came in and looked over every inch of this place. I had hired a guy with a history of sex crimes to do some painting for me the day Gina was taken. I just thought everyone deserves a second chance."

The man had a prior conviction for rape and gross sexual imposition. He has recently run afoul with the law again for not registering his whereabouts with authorities.

But he wasn't the only convicted sex offender within striking distance. Detectives looked closely at the parents of Gina's friends after her disappearance. One of her friend's stepfathers was arrested for having sex with an underage girl, according to the unnamed official. The day of Gina's disappearance, this man was working at a business within sight of the phone booth where Gina and a friend placed a call. He left work early that day and does not have a solid alibi, according to investigators.

> **"Certainly we've received some *information from psychics on these cases. We follow up on every lead."***

"We're looking at every possibility," says FBI spokesman Scott Wilson. "We are looking at the possibility that they are connected. Do we have a serial killer out there? But these cases might not be connected. So we're looking at unsolved sexual assaults, we're looking at unsolved missing person cases nationwide. We're looking at every possibility."

Cleveland detectives are currently taking a close look at convicted serial rapist Nathan Ford, who admitted to attacking girls and women in the Cleveland area for years. His victims range in age from 13 to 55, though he has not been linked to any murders. Ford was sentenced to 138 years in prison in 2006. Police want to know if he ever crossed paths with Gina.

Even leads from psychics are not dismissed. "The FBI usually does not work with psychics hand in hand. But certainly we've received some information from psychics on these cases. We take them. We follow up on every lead."

Felix DeJesus has heard from his share of psychics, too, but he stops listening when they say Gina must be dead. "It hurts," he says. "Just to hear someone say your daughter is dead. We try to block it out. Both of these girls are still alive. I'm convinced of that. Parents would feel that, if they were dead. If they were on the other side, we would know. I know she's not there. I don't feel her there."

Beth believes Mandy is still alive out there, too. "Until I know something else, I'm going to continue to believe that," she says. "But I'll listen to the psychics. I'll hear what they have to say."

Robin Dedeker claims she developed powers of second sight after her son committed suicide. She knows what it feels like to lose a child and the cases she works tend to be missing children. She wants to help reunite other families even if it is only with the body that remains. She wants to give closure even if it is not good news.

Like many of her readings, her vision of Mandy is disturbing.

"She's showing me this car," says Dedeker's voice, streaming out of the rickety cassette player. "There were three men. These three men were offering to party with her, to help her get a celebration on for her birthday. She knew these three men. Two of them are 18 or older. One of them is only 16 at the time all this is happening. They did go to the local high school.

"The 16-year-old is really struggling and having a hard time with the knowledge that he has to keep to himself. He's not a bad person but he's made some very bad choices. He has lots of nightmares about this night. The older two have dealt with what happened by blocking it out.

"The location where Amanda went with these three young men is somewhat isolated. It's a park. It's near the water. I'm seeing a kind of parking area. It's not real big. Off to one side is an overpass. There is water. Flowing water, a river. A few picnic tables. On the other side of the river I'm seeing big office buildings. This is Cleveland. I see a large tree.

"I'm seeing a driver pull out a bottle from under his seat. It's hard liquor. Whiskey. The driver takes a swig of it and passes it to Amanda. The driver is dark-skinned. He has black, short, curly hair. It's more of a little light wave curl to it. He's not a black man, he's Hispanic. Mixed Hispanic and white. The one that's sitting behind him is white and has sandy-brown hair. He's slightly built. The 16-year-old is skinny with brown hair. He's also white.

"Everyone is getting drunk fast. Pretty soon, there's some groping going on. The Hispanic man wants to have sex with Amanda."

The psychic goes on to describe, in graphic detail, how Mandy is taken from the vehicle, unconscious, slipping into shock from alcohol poisoning late in the night. The two older teens have sex with her. When they discover that she is not breathing they panic and fill her pockets with stones from the river bank, then roll her body into the Cuyahoga. There is an unspoken pledge that they will never tell anyone what happened.

Mandy's body, says Dedeker, is still in the river, caught in submerged tree branches.

"I'm being pointed to a location along Riverbed Street," Dedeker says. "Across the river is Sycamore Street. If you draw a line across Sycamore Street to the other side, that will give you an approximate location of where her body lies. It's very close to that point. Her body is deep enough that no one could see it from the surface and this is not an area where people swim. It will take professional divers and sonar equipment to locate her remains."

The psychic's lead will be categorized and added to the hundreds of pages of notes and interviews that have been gathered by FBI agents investigating the disappearance of Amanda Berry; boxes of leads, piled high inside a large room, next to boxes of tips related to Georgina DeJesus's abduction. This is long-term storage. Sharing the same room are boxes filled with the names of suspects in the unsolved abduction and murder of Amy Mihaljevic.

The Missing Children's Task Force is offering a $25,000 reward for information leading to the whereabouts of Amanda Berry and Georgina DeJesus or the murderer of Amy Mihaljevic. Anyone with information related to these cases should contact the Cleveland FBI at 216-522-1400, or the Cleveland Police Department at 216-621-1234.

CHAPTER 12

Amy: Through the Looking Glass

Still Searching for Amy Mihaljevic's Killer

Things would probably have turned out differently if I hadn't picked "bring your daughter to work day" to talk to the Accountant.

It was just one of those things. Another odd happenstance.

"Can you point me towards [the Accountant]?" I asked the receptionist, seated in the lobby of the single-floor firm. I used his real name, of course. But, since he remains an uncharged suspect, I am hesitant to put his name in print. As with other suspects listed in this chapter, I have excluded their names for their own protection so that over-eager do-gooders cannot harass those who are innocent.

"I don't know his extension," she said. "But his desk is right over here." The middle-aged woman started walking down a short corridor leading to rows of cubicles.

"I'll follow you," I said.

As we rounded a corner, I noticed for the first time that the office was teaming with middle school–aged girls. "It's 'bring your daughter to work day,'" the receptionist informed me. Anger, and fear—fear for them—started to brew inside me. There was no time for me to check myself.

"Here he is," the receptionist said, motioning toward a man sitting in front of a computer inside a tiny cubicle. He was skinny.

Somewhere in his 50s. His nose was misshapen from disease or an old wound. A young girl slid past him on her way to her mother's office door.

"Hello?" asked the Accountant.

"I'm James Renner," I said. "I've been looking for you."

At that, he sprung to his feet. "Get this man out of here, right now," he told the receptionist. But instead, she stood there, shocked.

I asked him if it was true that police had questioned him about Amy Mihaljevic.

"Don't say that name again," he warned.

"What? Amy Mihaljevic?"

He rushed at me, one hand up as if to punch me in the face. I backed away, quickly. I began to retreat to the door.

"Why don't you want to talk about Amy Mihaljevic?" I asked.

"Stop saying that name!" he shouted and ran toward me.

I headed for the door, a few strides ahead of him.

"Call the cops," he told the receptionist.

"Yes," I said. "Let's call the cops."

He stopped, panting. I turned around at the door.

"Leave," he said.

I obliged.

Amy was 10 when she disappeared from the idyllic West Side suburb of Bay Village. She was taken in front of a Baskin-Robbins ice cream store at the Bay Square shopping center, across the street from the police station, at about 2:30 P.M. on October 27, 1989. Her abductor was a well-dressed man with shaggy hair.

Amy had told friends she was meeting a man after school that day, a man who said he worked with her mother. The man had called Amy at home when she was alone in the house after school, and he had told her that her mother had just received a promotion. He said he wanted to take her shopping to pick out a present for her mom. He asked her to keep it a secret.

A jogger discovered Amy's body in a field just off County Road 1181, in Ashland County, on the morning of February 8, 1990. She

Amy is best known for the single ponytail she wore in her last class picture, but she usually wore her hair down, as in this earlier photograph. *(Mark Mihaljevic)*

had been stabbed in the neck and hit on the head with a blunt instrument.

We've never been told, definitively, if Amy had been sexually assaulted or how long her body had been in that field.

No one has been charged with her murder.

These clues were repeated over and over for years, on newscasts and in articles, until we could recite them by heart. But when I began investigating this crime in 2005, I was surprised at the amount of information about this case that had never been revealed to the public.

My motivation for delving into the mystery was simple and strange—I had fallen in love with Amy when I was 11. I fell in love with that image of her with the sidesaddle ponytail, and vowed to find her killer one day. In 1989, I spent weekends at Westgate Mall, looking for her. When I became a journalist as an adult, I decided to try my best to track down her killer, or at least keep her name in the spotlight.

In 2006, I wrote a book about my investigation, *Amy: My Search for Her Killer.* It introduces the lead detectives and FBI agents assigned to her case. It provides a minute-by-minute timeline of her last day. It offers a few new clues (the two eyewitnesses of the abduction never saw Amy get into a vehicle; gold fibers were found on Amy's body; there was some soy substance found in her stomach). It also debunks a few urban legends that have infected this case over time—no, Amy's family were not connected to the mob and they were never in witness protection.

The book's narrative ends as I peer into the window of a suspect's garage, inside what was once a small apartment attached to the back of the building. On the dirty burnt-orange carpet, I spy a dark stain that could be mud, or blood. For a moment, I consider committing a little breaking and entering, to procure a small sample, but I decide to obey the law and let the detectives do their job.

I was so certain it was him, the man I referred to in the book as "Mr. Harvey," a pseudonym borrowed from Alice Sebold's *The Lovely Bones.* William Gareau, the former police chief of Bay Village, told me that Mr. Harvey was on the top of his list, too. Mr. Harvey was the most interesting suspect I had discovered during the course of my research and I naively thought there were no other major suspects left to be found.

Detective Lieutenant Mark Spaetzel, the lead detective assigned to Amy's case, warned me there were "around 50 other people as compelling" as the suspects I had found. But I didn't believe him.

I was unprepared for the number of new leads people sent to me after the publication of the book. Leads that point to more interesting suspects than Mr. Harvey (although he remains on my short list). Leads that suggest the man who abducted Amy almost kidnapped another young girl from North Olmsted.

As more information continued to pour in (to the tune of 10 unique e-mails a day, on average) I began to question everything I thought I knew about the case. I can empathize with Alice, who ventured through the Looking Glass one day and found a world re-

Amy Mihaljevic's fifth-grade class photo became an iconic reminder of her mysterious abduction.

versed. This is a dark adventure leading into the shadows of society. And somewhere, lurking and watching (oh, always watching), is a Jabberwocky who knows my name.

Anyone who has spent significant time investigating the unsolved abduction and murder of Amy Mihaljevic is haunted by the 10-year-old girl. Some believe it is her ghost, a restless spirit whispering in their ears as they fall asleep, urging them onward, toward her killer. The skeptical detective may believe it is merely his own subconscious, demanding a solution. We complain about vivid nightmares. We feel her influence on our daily lives, in the shaping of mundane details and ordinary circumstance—that song on the radio that reminds us of a certain suspect, or the number 1181 (the number of the desolate road where her body was recovered) appearing on the license plate of a car that cuts us off on the highway. When we listen, especially on the anniversaries, we sometimes hear thoughts that are not our own.

I had my doubts. Until the psychic showed me the Polaroid she took of the dump site on County Road 1181, that is. The photo with the man's displaced face. Now, I don't kid myself. It's not my subconscious. Never was.

The psychic asked me to keep her identity secret, so I'll stick to first names. Sylvia called me at the newspaper one afternoon, shortly after the book was published. "I'm a seer," she said, and I rolled my eyes.

While researching Amy's case, I had made a conscious effort to avoid psychics. Soothsayers flock to unsolved abductions involving children and they are rarely helpful. Either they offer false hope, by telling the parents that their kid is still alive somewhere, or they crush the parents' spirits at a time they need to remain strong, by telling the details of their child's violent end. Many psychics wanted to talk to me about their visions of Amy's final moments. But I noticed that these so-called "psychics" who did track me down all had the same frantic intensity in their voices, an illogical excitement I've only ever heard in the voices of salesmen or cult leaders. And like salesmen and cult leaders, they usually stood to benefit financially if I did what they said, in their case, writing about their dreams in the paper.

But Sylvia didn't want publicity. She didn't want me to use her name. And when she spoke, there was no edginess in her voice. Instead, there was patience.

"I have something you should see," she said. "A couple things, really. The first is a photo album that was given to me by Amy's mother, Margaret. The second is a Polaroid that shows the face of Amy's killer."

I told her I'd be right over.

Amy's mom was a fascinating woman. She was a member of Mensa. She collected antique dictionaries. She also suffered from lupus, which was exacerbated by her alcoholism. Those who knew her describe a doting mother who was in love with her little girl,

Amy's parents, Margaret and Mark Mihaljevic, appeared on many TV programs, pleading for the kidnapper to return their daughter. *(The Morning Journal)*

but also stressed and preoccupied with the dissolution of her marriage in 1989. At the time of her kidnapping, Amy's parents were in the process of separating. I would have liked to talk with Margaret about her daughter. But her disease took her life in 2001. She died in her apartment in Las Vegas, where she had moved to be closer to her mother. Luckily, Margaret had been a shutterbug. She documented the lives of her two children—Amy, and her older brother Jason—in a collection of photo albums, organized by year. Before moving to Vegas, she gave the most important album to Sylvia for safe keeping.

Sylvia had driven to the Mihaljevic house shortly after Amy was taken and introduced herself to the family. Something about this particular psychic must have impressed Margaret, because Sylvia was the only one she ever used.

The psychic's home was decorated in what I would call Midwestern Grandma. Pictures of family propped on every exposed surface; cotton tablecloth in the dining room; brick-a-brack displayed for your viewing pleasure. We sat at the dining room table and she produced an ancient-looking, cloth-bound photo album. I opened it up and understood immediately why this specific album was the most important one Margaret had owned—inside was a lock of Amy's hair.

The series of thoughts that danced in my head in the seconds following this discovery may provide a better look into my own psyche than I'm particularly comfortable with. My first thought was cloning. I'm a sci-fi nerd, after all. I know it'll be possible in my lifetime to clone a human being. And what better human to clone than one whose original life was cut short, unfairly? Is that a frightening thought? Selfishly naïve and immature? Just a little *too* crazy? Yeah, okay. Probably, it is. But my next thought was even more dangerous. My next thought was simply: *This is evidence. Evidence that could be planted in a suspect's house.*

No, this photo album wasn't just important. It was a ticking time bomb. I quickly realized that the only people who should ever have it in their possession is Amy's family. It cannot be trusted to anyone else. I didn't even trust myself to deliver it to Amy's dad, so I contacted him and asked that he drive directly to Sylvia's house to retrieve it ASAP. I'm happy to report he did just that.

I set the album aside and asked to see the Polaroid.

Sylvia handed me a standard Polaroid photograph. It showed the familiar rise of earth where Amy's body was discovered in a wheat field off CR 1181. The picture was taken only a day or two after the body was recovered; the dirt had been scraped for evidence and a temporary memorial had been arranged by grieving community members who had left behind teddy bears and flowers.

"I have a magnifying glass if you need it," she said.

"I don't," I answered.

There it was. Plain as day. Near the center of the frame was a man's face, in the shadows and highlights formed by the dirt. It was not something you needed to squint to see. It wasn't something you needed to imagine into existence, like those 3-D puzzle pictures that were so popular at mall kiosks a couple of years ago. In the dirt was a man's face, in very minute detail. The man was balding. He had a large nose. He looked vaguely like the composite sketch of Amy's abductor, but older.

"In 1989, I thought that was the killer's face as he looked, then," said Sylvia, as if picking the thought out of my mind. "But I came to understand that this is the face of the killer, as he will look when he is finally caught. It's the face of the killer as he looks, today."

But he didn't look like anyone I had met.

Was it the face of the Jabberwocky? Whoever it is, he has had cameos in my nightmares ever since.

If there was a nemesis in my search for answers in Amy's case, it was a woman named Karen Emery, the wife of the Ashland County coroner.

The details of Amy's autopsy were never made public after her murder. William Emery, the coroner in charge of it, went to great lengths to hide it from the media. He went so far as to wait an entire year after Amy's body was found in his jurisdiction before completing her official death certificate, which, he knew, would be available to reporters at the county's bureau of vital statistics.

Although his wife is not on the county payroll, Karen answers phones at the coroner's office inside the new Justice Center. Due to state nepotism laws, she must remain an unpaid employee. However, there's no doubt she is in charge in Ashland County. She refused to give me access, she said, because "I don't trust reporters."

At the time the book was published, Karen and Ashland County Prosecutor Ramona Rogers had me caught in a macabre Catch-22. They could not release the autopsy report, they said, because the documents did not exist inside Ashland County. In fact, it was the Cuyahoga County Coroner's Office that had conducted Amy's autopsy in 1990, because Ashland didn't have the proper facilities and manpower to handle it. So, the records have always been kept in Cuyahoga County. But then–Cuyahoga County coroner Dr. Elizabeth Balraj could not release the records to me without the permission of William Emery. And Mr. Emery would not grant his permission.

I contacted the ACLU, the attorney general's office, the state's coroners association, and finally Terry Gilbert, the attorney who represented Sam Sheppard's son in the most recent trial. Threatening letters were sent, but the Emerys didn't blink. Karen retaliated by demanding that the Ashland University bookstore take down a display of my book. I figured that I would just have to wait until Mr. Emery retired or finally keeled over and try again with the next coroner. I'm a young man, after all. And he is very old.

Then, one afternoon, my wife Julie came home from school. She teaches high school choir in Akron. As usual, she went through the events of her day—which students were making progress, which students were being royal pains in the ass, etc. One of her students was working on logic puzzles. Mind teasers. And one of these puzzles lodged itself in my brain like a viral worm and kept repeating and repeating for hours. It was the one about the goat and the cabbage and the wolf and the boat.

So there's this goat and a cabbage and a wolf and a boat. And what you have to do is figure out a way to get each of the items onto the boat and across the pond to an island, without the wolf eating the goat or the goat eating the cabbage. The trick is, you can only keep one item in the boat at a time. The solution, like all good mind teasers, is elegantly simple—you take the goat to the island, then come back for the cabbage, then return to the island and drop off the cabbage, where you place the goat *back* in the boat, row to the mainland again, drop off the goat, pick up the wolf, take the wolf to the island, then return, at last, for the goat.

Thinking of this puzzle, it dawned on me how I might get my hands on Amy's autopsy report.

I called Dr. Balraj. "Can you make a copy of the entire autopsy report?" I asked. "Everything you have related to Amy's case, actually."

"Mr. Renner, I cannot release that information to you without Emery's approval," she said.

"The copies aren't for me," I explained. "I want you to copy the report, then send it to Emery in Ashland County."

Dr. Balraj agreed to do me this favor. And as soon as I knew the documents were in Ashland County, I requested them again. This time, they were forced to let me see the report.

Amy's body was found 10 feet from the road on CR 1181 in a desolate corner of Ashland County. The FBI believes the killer was familiar with this location. *(The Ashland Times Gazette)*

"No pens, no pencils, no paper, no recording devices of any kind, and we won't copy anything for you," Karen told me before letting me inside the coroner's office. "You can sit next to me and read it."

An old Chinese curse came to mind as I opened the file: *Be careful what you wish for. You just might get it.*

I wish I could unsee the photographs of the crime scene. I'd rather remember Amy as the bright-eyed girl in that school picture. I'll not go into detail. However, there are some definitive answers in the autopsy report that are worth noting:

- Amy's body was in the field for a long time before it was discovered by that morning jogger. A little seedling had actually grown through her pants leg.
- There is evidence suggesting Amy was murdered at a separate location and her body stored there for a short period of time before being moved to the field. A day or two. A week at most. Wherever it was, her body had been kept relatively cool and away from insects. It could have been stored in a cabin or a garage or a trunk.

- The material in her stomach was never identified. Contrary to rumor, it could have been what she had for lunch that Friday. Or it could have been a meal the killer fed to her after her abduction. It looks like it could have been pizza, actually, which was on the school menu the afternoon she was taken, so I, personally, lean toward that answer. And if it *is* school pizza, then she must have been killed shortly after being abducted, since it was not fully digested.
- There is evidence of a sexual assault.
- Amy's underwear was inside-out, which suggests the killer may have redressed her after she was dead.
- There is a distinct possibility that DNA evidence was collected from Amy's body.
- Her nails were damaged, perhaps as she fought against her attacker. I'd like to think she got a few good licks in, at least.

When I was through, I put the file back on Karen's desk and turned to leave.

"Wait," she said.

What now?

"Will you sign my book?" she asked.

I smiled. "Can I borrow a pen?"

Factual accounts have a half-life. They degrade into myth, rumor, and legend over time, especially in high-profile cases like this. The more time separates a reporter from an event, the more difficult it is for us to sift through the junk for the few grains of truth that still remain untold.

One of the rumors that kept resurfacing during my research was: "the man who abducted Amy called a bunch of girls in North Olmsted, too." These girls, if they really existed, have never been named. They have never talked to reporters. I couldn't think of any way to verify this claim while writing the book. But as soon as the book was published, they contacted me.

So far, I've heard from eight young women who claim to have

Amy's ashes are buried beneath those of her mother in West Berlin, Wisconsin.

been called by Amy's killer, in 1989, when they were 10 or 11 years old. Of those, four can be chalked up to other perverts who used phone lines to get off in the age before Internet chat rooms. Of the four that remain, three lived in North Olmsted. One lived in Bay Village.

One of the women from North Olmsted, "Ms. C," told me the man had called her at home and asked her to meet him around the corner from her house so she could go with him to the store to buy a present for her mom. She was heading out the door when a neighbor stopped her and asked where she was going. Luckily, the neighbor kept the girl home, sensing something was amiss, and alerted her parents. A week later, Amy was taken.

The police and FBI know about these girls. After Amy vanished, their parents (and the parents of a half dozen other girls) were given directions to a building in Bay Village (perhaps the community center, behind the town hall) where they met one evening to talk about the case, in secret. There, detectives and special agents interviewed the girls to determine how they were all connected. The killer must have known them all. He knew when the girls were home alone and he knew their telephone numbers—in at least one case, the number was unlisted.

There are a few ways in which these girls' lives overlapped with Amy's. Many of them took horse riding lessons at area stables, including Holly Hill, Senoj Stables, and Blueridge Stables. One girl even had the same female instructor as Amy. They all visited flea markets in the fall of 1989. And they all visited Lake Erie Nature and Science Center. The nature center is on Wolf Road, in Bay Village.

> *It seemed that an arrest was imminent. But, for reasons that still remain unclear, an arrest was never made.*

Amy went there all the time. (I donated 10% of what I earned off the book to the center, in her memory). Children visiting the nature center often signed their names and phone numbers on a ledger of guests that the museum kept displayed in the main hallway. A leading theory is that Amy and the girls from North Olmsted put their personal information onto this ledger, and the kidnapper copied it onto a separate piece of paper to use later.

Around Saint Patrick's Day, 2005, several of these women received a phone call from an FBI agent who worked on the case. One woman's parents were awakened by a phone call in their cabin on a cruise ship in the middle of the Caribbean. The caller wanted to confirm that they had all visited the nature center. It seemed that an arrest was imminent. But, for reasons that still remain unclear, an arrest was never made.

One of the young women called me directly after she read my book. "There's a name in here that is familiar to me," said "Ms. J." "It's the last name of Amy's riding instructor. It's such an uncommon last name, but there was a man who taught math at North Olmsted who had the same name. I wonder if they're related."

I checked it out. Sure enough, the math teacher is the brother of Amy's riding instructor. And he sometimes visited his sister at the horse stables. He was never questioned by investigators in 1989.

I immediately turned that lead over to Bay Village and the FBI. It was a name they had not had before. But I've heard nothing more on the subject.

These women still wonder who the man was, and how close they came to ending up like Amy.

.   .   .

The most common question I'm asked, of course, is: "Who do you think did it?"

I don't know. What's frustrating is the number of men who had the opportunity to commit this crime.

The FBI has a "Top 25" list. In December 2006, Bay Village police asked about six men to give DNA samples. All but one complied. In my opinion, Amy's killer is probably one of the following five men.

The Accountant

Another rumor surrounding the case is that "an accountant is involved."

In 1989, a Cleveland police officer who worked sex crimes was given a tip by a prostitute-informant. The woman said that just before Amy was abducted, she had been contacted by one of her regular johns, who had asked her to find him a 10- or 11-year-old girl. He wanted to wrap her in plastic and defecate on her. Cleveland police detectives followed him for weeks—he lived in a house on the west side with his mother and worked in the city as an accountant for a large firm. Before work, he often stopped by area middle schools and watched the girls walking to class.

After the composite sketch was released to the public, the Accountant cut his hair very short. Sometimes, the detectives would sit next to him at McDonald's and watch him methodically eat his fries one by one, wiping the grease off his hands after each bite.

They noticed that the Accountant kept his attic window open, odd behavior for such an anal man, especially in the middle of winter. They wondered if Amy's body was being kept there, the window left open for ventilation. It was enough for a search warrant. But, to the detectives' chagrin, the lead FBI agent assigned to the case refused to execute the warrant.

We'll never know what the Accountant was keeping in his attic— a fire destroyed the house some years later. The cause of the fire was determined to be "arson." The Accountant blamed local kids. After Amy's body was found, the Accountant went to Amy's funeral service and gave Amy's mother an envelope with $1,000 inside. "In my gut, I've always believed it was him," says one retired detective, on the condition of anonymity.

The Boarder

A man with a shady past boarded his horse at Holly Hill, where Amy took lessons. He had a prior conviction for statutory rape in the state of Washington and was busted for fleeing the state and moving to Ohio, in 1989. His father worked at the courthouse here, and whether that had anything to do with it, he got off lightly, for a fugitive. For a while he a drove truck, but he retired on disability a few years ago. Girls at Holly Hill and Senoj Stables, where he moved his horse, recall the Boarder as a pervert who liked to tickle little girls. One girl, now a grown woman, claims he once drove her to Ashland County when she was a young teen. He promised to let her ride a horse down there, but the girl made him turn around after he tried to kiss her. He denies this event took place. Another woman, who knew him at Senoj, says that she once bumped into him in line at the grocery store. She had to use her driver's license to write a check and feels he must have memorized her address to look up in a cross-reference directory later, because that night he started calling her on the phone, asking her to meet him, even though she had never given him her number.

The Teacher

The brother of Amy's riding instructor is the one man who knew each of the girls from North Olmsted who received creepy calls in October 1989. He retired in 2006 and currently lives in Rocky River. He has no prior criminal record that I could find. But his self-evaluations contained inside his file at the school where he taught gave me goosebumps. In 1987, he told his principal that he was going to copy his students' personal information onto note cards that he could take home with him, explaining that this would allow him to reach their parents on a more regular basis.

·   ·   ·

Volunteers distributed hundreds of thousands of copies of Amy's missing poster with these illustrations in November and December 1989. The poster generated leads from as far away as Australia.

The Artist

I met with the Artist in February of 2008, after learning of his identity via an anonymous e-mail. He lives on the West Side, off Lorain Avenue, and agreed to meet me at a coffee shop around the corner from his house. I was struck by his uncanny resemblance to the composite sketch of Amy's abductor. He must have noticed it, too, because he once took a poster of Amy's killer, punched out the eyeballs, and wore it as a mask to work. In 1989, the Artist was employed by the Metroparks, but prior to that he taught art classes at Emerson Middle School in Lakewood and Bay Village High School. He readily admits that when he was a teacher he invited female students back to his place, but he maintains this only happened "after they graduated." In the fall of 1989, he worked on a couple of small projects at the Lake Erie Nature and Science Center. He also bowled regularly in the Bay Square bowling alley. He probably crossed paths with Amy during that time, though he says they never met. A check of his personnel records at the Metroparks shows he did not show up for work the day Amy was abducted, even though he was scheduled to. When questioned by the FBI in 1989, he told them that he couldn't remember what he had done that day. When we met, the Artist wanted to show me a collage of pictures he had constructed from photos of a twenty-something Internet stripper he had befriended. Among the photos was the image of a prepubescent girl, whom he identified as his niece. I told him I thought it was strange that he lived so close to where Amanda Berry and Gina DeJesus were abducted. "You know what's strange?" he said. "I *knew* Amanda Berry." He said that Mandy's best friend was his neighbor and that they had come to his house one day to "party." But the friend, when contacted by the FBI, denied she knew Amanda Berry. He later claimed that he wasn't really sure that it was the missing girl who had been in his house.

The Shaggy-Haired Man

The Shaggy-Haired Man hits the trifecta of circumstantial links to the abduction/murder of Amy Mihaljevic: he volunteered at the Lake Erie Nature and Science Center in 1989, he lived at his parents' house in New London (less than five minutes from where her body was found), and he strongly resembles the composite sketch of Amy's abductor. The Shaggy-Haired Man was once a teacher in the Amherst/Vermilion area. Several students I've spoken to say he occasionally took them back to his room, or out to eat, though all say nothing sexual took place when they were alone. Though he was a teacher throughout the '70s, '80s, and '90s, there is a period of two years between 1987 and 1989 when he simply disappeared. The story he told co-workers was that he had contracted a rare blood disease and believed he was going to die. He told friends he spent that time traveling the world. In 1989, he returned to Lorain County and resumed teaching until investigators, acting on a fresh tip, began questioning his relatives in 2003. At that time, the Shaggy-Haired Man abruptly quit his job and moved out of state.

Authorities are still offering a $25,000 reward to the person who can solve this case. Anyone with information should contact the Bay Village Police Department at 440-871-1234 or the Cleveland FBI office at 216-522-1400. I will continue to update this case at www.amymihaljevic.blogspot.com, and you can reach me, directly, at jamesrenner@grayco.com

CHAPTER 13

The Serial Killer's Apprentice

The Assuredly Unsolved Murders of
Krista Harrison, Tina Harmon, and Debbie Smith

The march to the Death House is silent.

Phil Trexler makes his way across the parking lot with the rest of the media, walking quietly along, imagining what comes next. Trexler is there as a representative of the *Akron Beacon Journal.* He has written about the man, Robert Buell, the rapist, the *child* killer, for the paper. And he has come here, to Lucasville, to watch him die.

The Death House is separated from the visitors' center—where a nice spread of fresh danish and coffee was set out for the reporters as they waited—but the walk is not long enough. And as Trexler passes the funeral director's car, the gravity of the moment sinks in.

Trexler and the other reporters are ushered into the Death House, into a small room bisected by a partition. Three men sit on one side, holding hands. This is the family of Krista Harrison, who was abducted, raped, and murdered in 1982, when she was 11 years old. This is her father and her brothers. On the other side of the partition is Buell's attorney, Patricia Millhoff, and his pastor, Ernie Sanders. The reporters can stand on either side of the room, but the partition is there so the victim's family does not have to make eye contact with those who have come to support the murderer in his final moments. Everyone faces the front, where a glass window overlooks an empty gurney.

On the other side of the glass, someone closes a curtain, obscuring the hospital bed for a moment.

Patricia Millhoff begins to cry. Ten minutes ago, she had to tell Buell that his stay of execution had not been granted. Buell had prepared for this—he'd already had his "special meal," the single, unpitted olive—but Millhoff had been hoping for some luck. She'd gotten to know Buell well since becoming part of his legal team, fighting to overturn his conviction. As the appeals process fizzled out and the execution date drew closer, her visits with Buell had become less about law and more about simple human interaction. They usually discussed the morning's Diane Rehm show or what books Buell was currently reading into a recorder for blind people. After the prison refused to allow Buell to donate his typewriter to other inmates, he willed it away to Millhoff, along with his TV.

Ernie Sanders, Buell's pastor, believes he knows who really killed Krista.

"If you did it, and you admit it, it will help everybody," she had told him, in private.

"I didn't do it," he had replied.

The curtain opens. Buell is there, now, lying on the gurney. He is strapped down, facing the ceiling. His shirt is tucked in. He appears calm. An IV tube snakes out of his arm. The tube disappears behind a wall, where the executioner stands, waiting for the signal.

Trexler watches Buell's Adam's apple bob up and down. Up and down. Counting off the last seconds like a swallowed metronome. The reporter is struck by the absurdity of a healthy man being led into a room to die.

In the Death House, it remains silent except for the sound of the reporters' pencils scribbling notes on pads of paper.

Sitting there, Ernie Sanders, Buell's pastor, believes he knows who really killed Krista. It's something they've talked about at length. "You were right all along," Buell told him the last time they met.

Eyewitnesses provided a description of Krista's abductor. They said his hair curled at the ends. *(Wayne County Prosecutor's Office)*

Seventeen years earlier Buell had written to Sanders and asked him to visit to talk about forgiveness. Buell had a lot to confess—the rapes of two women, at least—but Sanders's God has grace enough for that. Grace enough to forgive even the murder of the child, he told Buell. But Buell had never confessed to that one. And in Sanders's mind, he didn't have to.

It is time for last words. Buell has some for Krista's family. "Jerry and Shirley, I didn't kill your daughter," he says, even though Shirley is not there. "The prosecutor knows that . . . and they left the real killer out there on the streets to kill again and again and again."

When Buell is done, some unseen signal is given on the other side of the glass. Trexler notices a change in Buell's breathing. He watches Buell close his eyes and watches his chest heave up and down and watches his Adam's apple finally stop and then there is total silence.

It is September 24, 2002. After 18 years on death row, Robert Buell is dead.

Later, when the Death House is empty again, Buell's typewriter goes home with Millhoff. His personal collection of court transcripts, police files, letters, and handwritten notes leaves with Sanders. That box of documents, in time, finds its way to me.

The box is full of secrets.

Evidence found inside suggests a strange possibility: that Buell was telling the truth when he said he didn't kill Krista Harrison. And that he knew who did.

In the early 1980s, someone was killing little girls in Ohio.

The first incident appeared to be the abduction and murder of 12-year-old Tina Harmon in the fall of 1981. Tina was a cute, round-faced girl from the small town of Creston with shoulder-length hair and a taste for Camel Light cigarettes. Back then, the only real entertainment was the game room at the Union 76 truck stop in Lodi, a few miles away. Tina was known to hang out there whenever she could hitch a ride.

According to police reports, on Thursday, October 29, 1981, Tina got a ride into town from her father's girlfriend, who dropped her off in front of a convenience store with a group of friends. Tina bought a Fudgesicle and bummed another ride from her teenage brother, who took her only as far as the next Lawson's. Eventually, she made it to Lodi; several witnesses, including a local detective, remembered seeing her there that evening. Tina was last spotted in the presence of an unshaven man in a jean jacket, who appeared to be in his early 20s.

The girl's body was found five days later in Bethlehem Township, about 40 miles from her home, dumped beside an oil well in plain sight of anyone driving down the road. She was fully clothed and had been placed neatly on the ground. She'd been raped and strangled shortly after she was abducted. Oil well workers who had visited that access road the day before had seen nothing, and this supported the detectives' theory that Tina's body had been stored someplace else before being placed in the field.

In her pocket they found a book of matches from the Union 76 truck stop. On her clothes, the coroner found dog hair and several "trilobal polyester" fibers the color of nutmeg.

Less than a year later—July 17, 1982, a stormy Saturday—Krista Harrison was snatched from a baseball field across the street from her home. She had been collecting cans with a 12-year-old friend, Roy, who later told police that around 5 P.M., a dark-colored van pulled into the park. The van had bubble-shaped windows, black seats, and a roof vent.

The driver climbed out and approached Krista. The man was white and looked to be about 25 to 35 years old. He was skinny, with a mustache and dark brown hair that curled near his shoulders; he looked Italian, the boy thought. The man said something to Krista and she went and sat on the bleachers overlooking the diamond. The man then sat down next to the girl and reached underneath her blouse. When Krista started to cry, the man whispered something into her ear. Roy could not hear what was said, but Krista walked to the man's van, opened the driver's-side door, climbed between the front bucket seats and sat on the floor. The man climbed in, too, and then leaned out the window. "Bye, Roy," he said. He pulled the van onto the road and quickly sped away.

When Krista started to cry, the man whispered something into her ear.

Witnesses later said that a strange man resembling Krista's abductor had attended one of her summer softball games, photographing her with a 35 mm camera. Classmates told police that on the afternoon Krista was abducted, she had gone to the Village Snack Shop game room and when she left, a strange man had blocked her way and tried to get her to dance with him. The man had dark hair that was curly on the ends.

And in the weeks leading up to her abduction, there had been several prank calls placed to the Harrison residence when Krista was home.

Krista was missing for less than a week. On July 23, two turtle trappers discovered her body next to an abandoned shed in a field in nearby Holmes County. She was fully clothed and wrapped in plastic. The coroner discovered carpet fibers on her, the same trilobal polyester fibers that had been found on Tina Harmon. Like Tina,

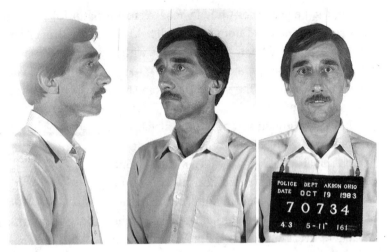

Robert Buell, age 42, at the time of arrest in 1983. *(Summit County Sheriff's Department)*

Krista had been strangled to death shortly after being kidnapped and her body had been stored in a fly-free environment—a trunk of a car, or a van—before being moved to the field. Like Tina, she had been sexually assaulted, possibly with a vibrator.

The next day, a second crime scene was located in West Salem. In the weeds next to the road, police found a green plastic garbage bag covered in Krista's blood and hair. Beside the bag was a Budweiser blanket and pieces of blood-stained cardboard.

Then, a second sweep of the area where Krista's body had been found turned up a pair of dirty jeans, spotted with blood and specks of powder-blue paint. There was a hole in the left knee. A man's plaid shirt was also found.

The evidence was sent to the crime lab at the Bureau of Criminal Identification and Investigation, which determined that the plastic bag that Krista was wrapped in and the cardboard box found at the second scene had once contained van seats that had been ordered through Sears. On the bag was a fingerprint.

Sears provided detectives with the names of everyone in the area who had ordered similar seats. The list was long, but every name was checked out. Bob Buell was on the list and was interviewed, but the detective did not feel that Buell was being deceptive and so he did not become the focus of their investigation.

The FBI commissioned a criminal profile of the perpetrator by Special Agent John Douglas, whose pioneering studies of the habits of serial killers inspired the book *The Silence of the Lambs*. Krista's killer should be in his early to late 20s, Douglas said. He is a latent homosexual.

"When employed, he seeks menial or unskilled trades," wrote Douglas. "While he considers himself a 'macho man,' he has deep-rooted feelings of personal inadequacies. Your offender has a maximum of a high school education. When he is with children, he feels superior, in control, nonthreatened. While your offender may not be from the city where the victim was abducted he certainly has been there many times before (i.e., visiting friends, relatives, employment). He turned towards alcohol and/or drugs to escape from the realities of the crime."

Detectives from several jurisdictions and FBI special agents worked diligently to find the man who killed Krista and Tina. But the evidence could not be matched to a likely suspect, and each new lead only led them to a different dead end.

And then it happened again.

On Saturday, June 25, 1983, 10-year-old Debbie Smith disappeared from a street fair in Massillon. Later that day, Debbie called home. She sounded upset but would not say where she was. On August 6, a canoeist found Debbie's body on the banks of the Tuscarawas River. She had been raped. She had most likely been stabbed, although the body also showed signs of blunt force trauma. Melted wax was found on her body, and the candles from which it had come were recovered nearby.

These murders were still on the minds of police and area residents two months later when Franklin Township police received a chilling call from a Doylestown resident. There was a shaved, naked woman with a handcuff attached to one wrist standing in her kitchen, the caller said. The woman had shown up on her doorstep, claiming that she had been held captive in the house across the street—a little ranch house owned by Bob Buell.

The victim was a 28-year-old woman from Salem. She worked at a gas station, and on the night of October 16, 1983, she had been painting the office floor when a middle-aged man came up behind her with a gun and ordered her into his van. He pushed her between the front seats and handcuffed her hands behind her back. Then he drove her to his house, into an attached garage, and told her to go into the bedroom and undress. Inside, the man handcuffed her to a leather bench and spent the rest of the night raping, torturing, and degrading the woman in increasingly vile and unique ways. When it was over, he shaved her head and tied her to his bed. In the morning he went to work, promising to return around lunchtime.

Other women came forward claiming they had been abducted and raped by him, then released.

But the woman escaped, and when Buell returned home, a Franklin Township cop was waiting. Buell was arrested and charged with multiple counts of rape and kidnapping.

At the time, Buell was 42 years old. He had a college degree and was employed by the city of Akron, writing loans for the Planning Department. He was dating an attorney. He had a daughter at Kent State. Those who knew him described a neat, clean, orderly man, almost to the point of obsessive-compulsive disorder.

He didn't exactly fit the FBI's profile of their child killer. But when other agencies got word of Buell's arrest and recognized his name from the list of men who had purchased van seats from Sears, police descended upon his home with an array of search warrants. They found everything they were looking for, and more.

In a guest bedroom, painted powder-blue, detectives discovered a roll of carpet the color of nutmeg. The fibers were trilobal polyester and matched fibers found on the bodies of Tina Harmon and Krista Harrison. In the closet were jeans with a hole worn into the left knee. The pants were the same size and brand as the pair found near Krista's body. They also found dog hairs that matched those found on Tina, a newspaper clipping on the abduction of Debbie Smith, and candles of the same brand that were found near Debbie's body.

Investigators took Buell's van, too, a 1978 maroon Dodge with new black seats from Sears. Inside was more of that same nutmeg carpeting.

Police put Buell's picture into a lineup which was shown to witnesses. Several people who had attended Krista's last softball game identified Buell as a stranger they saw watching the game. A check of Buell's time cards revealed he had taken time off from work the day Krista's body was dumped.

As Buell's face became a front-page and TV news staple, other women came forward claiming they had been abducted and raped by him, then released. One woman from West Virginia told a grim story almost identical to the Salem victim's, down to being handcuffed in the bedroom so that Buell could go to work.

But all of these women were in their late 20s or older. So FBI Special Agent Bill Callis commissioned a second criminal profile to help explain what is referred to in his report as "the missing link" between Buell's practice of raping and releasing grown women and his presumed taste for raping and killing young girls. Serial killers tend to stick to one sex and age group and tend to escalate in violence over time; they generally don't start just letting victims go. This second report was not prepared by John Douglas, but by another profiler in the FBI's Behavioral Science Unit. It blamed Buell's mother.

Buell pleaded no contest to the rape charges and was sentenced to 121 years in prison for those crimes. He was only charged with one murder, Krista's, even though police believed he had also murdered Tina Harmon and Debbie Smith and maybe more. But as one detective put it, "How many times do you need to kill a man?" Buell was convicted of Krista's murder on April 4, 1984. The jury sentenced him to die.

Martin Frantz was assistant prosecutor for Wayne County during Buell's lengthy trial and played a significant role in sending the Akron city employee to the Death House. Today, Frantz is county prosecutor and remembers the case well, down to the names of eyewitnesses, 23 years later. He has no doubt that Buell killed those girls.

"It wasn't in the trial," he says, "but we had someone figure out, mathematically, how many people in the world could possibly be connected to all of that circumstantial evidence that we found inside Buell's home. It was something like 1 in 6 trillion."

Actually, it's at least 2 in 6 trillion.

Bob Buell was not living at his ranch house during the summer of 1982, when Krista was abducted. His nephew was. Ralph Ross Jr. was a skinny 20-year-old from Mingo Junction, a factory town just outside Steubenville. He had dark hair that curled near his shoulders and was growing a mustache. In February 1982, Ross moved to Akron to drive a truck for an auto parts manufacturer. His uncle Bob let him stay in the powder-blue guest room. Usually Ross had the house to himself because Buell spent most nights at his girlfriend's place. In exchange for room and board, Ross did chores around the house. It was his job to bag and take out the garbage.

Ross was Buell's ex-wife's brother's kid, but they shared a special kinship that was thicker than blood. For instance, they plotted to kidnap women and "do things" to them inside Buell's van.

"What are some of those things?" asked Wayne County Sheriff's Department Detective Dennis Derflinger, in an interview with Ross, shortly after Buell's arrest in 1983.

"Tying them up, shaving their crotch, putting a gag in their mouth, using a vibrator, that's about all," said Ross.

Ross went into a little more detail about these conversations when questioned by Frantz in front of a grand jury.

"Can you tell us what you remember about what Robert Buell said when he was talking of these fantasies and riding around in the van?" asked Frantz.

"I would like to say something," Ross replied. "It was me as well as him that was discussing whatever we were discussing."

Frantz: "So both of you were talking about it?"

Ross: "It was a two-way conversation."

Frantz: "Just tell us what Buell said."

Ross: "Well, he would talk about, if we would pass up a girl or something on the street, talked about 'wouldn't it be nice to have that girl for this evening,' and I would say, 'yeah, sure would.'"

Frantz: "What else was said?"

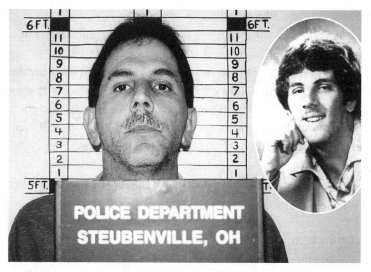

Ralph Ross after his arrest for drug possession in 2007. Inset: His 1979 senior class photo. *(Steubenville Police Department)*

Ross: "Well, I said I would doubt if she would go out with me or get together, that I didn't know her, just passed her up on the street. And he said well—or we both suggested—that we could get her into the van if we wanted to."

Ross specifically remembered cruising Marshallville, where Krista lived.

When Ross moved into Buell's house, the roll of nutmeg carpet was still being stored in the living room, where it had been for years. It matched the color of Buell's old van, a golden-brown 1977 Dodge that Buell had sold to Ross in 1980 and which Ross was still driving that summer of 1982. That van and Buell's new one were very similar, but Ross's had a sun roof and bubble windows. And Ross's van was a little dirtier; Buell had let his daughter's dog sleep in it before selling it to Ross.

But they didn't just share seats and vans, they shared women, too. Women like Buell's secretary.

Frantz: "And the three of you were in bed together?"

Ross: "Yes."

Frantz: "And at that time the vibrator was used?"

Ross: "Me and Bob both used it."

Ross's hair was a little curly and Buell's was straight, but otherwise the two shared an uncanny resemblance. In fact, when a police officer responded to a noise violation at the house in July 1982, he mistook Ross for Buell. (Ross may have shown him Buell's driver's license.) And a closer look at original interviews with bystanders at Krista's last softball game raises important questions as well. One who identified Buell in a lineup also said, "There was another man standing beside him with a camera and mirrored sunglasses on."

The detective asked her if she meant that it was Buell who was taking photographs.

"No, the man beside him was taking photographs. [Buell] did not have a camera."

Roy, the boy who stood just a few feet away from Krista's abductor when she was taken, said repeatedly that the man he saw that day was not Buell, but that the man was similar in appearance.

Ross did not have an alibi for the day Krista was abducted. He told police that he was probably visiting his parents that weekend, but couldn't remember for sure, and this apparently was never confirmed. Detective Derflinger asked Ross to submit fingerprints and his photo, but he refused. Derflinger ends his written report with this observation: "P.S. He has started to grow a beard, but I don't think that means anything."

When interviewed by Franklin Township Detective Ron Fuchs about whether Ross had ever helped Buell alter his vans, Ross was more evasive. "Ralph's answers are contrary to other information already gained and he appeared to be deliberately lying and trying to cover up the incident," Fuchs stated. In fact, Ross had helped his uncle move seats from Ross's old van—the one he was still driving—into Buell's new van.

A witness told police that he saw the jeans and shirt that were found at one of Krista's crime scenes lying near the road at around 11:30 the morning of July 23. Police believe Krista's body also must have been dumped that morning because the items strewn about the road were not seen before then. The jeans and shirt are assumed to have been dumped at the same time. But Buell was at work until noon that day. And, according to his girlfriend, the only reason he took the rest of the day off was to help her fix her clothes dryer. She produced a receipt that showed she had purchased a dryer belt that afternoon. By the time Buell had a chance to stop by his house, it was 4:50 P.M. In a letter to the Rev. Sanders during his incarceration, Buell stated that he remembered the time because he thought it was odd that his nephew was home so early on a work day, and that Ross's hand was wrapped in bandages. "He told me he had injured his hand at work and had to go to the hospital to get his hand x-rayed and bandaged," wrote Buell. Ross's employer had no record of the injury, according to police reports. Buell's girlfriend also told police that the last time she saw the boxes that had contained the van seats they were in the garage next to the garbage cans, where they waited for Ross to take them out to the curb on collection day.

A week after Krista's body was found, a year before anyone was implicated in the crime, Ross abruptly quit his job in Akron and moved back home to Mingo Junction. He went to work at his mother's craft store and, for a while, managed small booths for her at area malls, flea markets, and street fairs.

And then there is the evidence that detectives didn't find. When they confiscated Buell's van, they vacuumed every inch of its interior but did not find one hair or fiber from Tina Harmon, Krista Harrison, or Debbie Smith. As any good detectives knows, when an object makes contact with another object, a transfer of material always occurs. They never bothered to test Ross's van. The fingerprint on the plastic bag does not match Buell's. DNA collected at the crime scenes did not match Buell, either. No one attempted to match this material to Ross.

During the five months he lived in Akron, Ross made a few friends on Symphony Lane. Guys he smoked dope with. They were interviewed by police, too, but didn't appear to have much to say at the time. I re-interviewed those friends for this story, in 2007. One of them, a man named Carl Calvert, called me back after he had some time to think over the events of the summer of '82.

"Dead cells have awakened," he said. "At the time, when all this went down . . ."

Suddenly, over the phone line, I heard what sounded, at first, like a woman screaming.

"Molly, please!" yelled Calvert, and the screaming stopped. "That's my parrot," he explained.

After a moment, he continued.

"I briefly did suspect Ralph. If he wasn't involved, he knew of it. He was home all the time when it happened. Their vans were very similar. But Ross's had wooden cup holders and there were always roaches in the ashtray, if you know what I mean. But since police didn't do anything about him back then, I figured he must not have done anything."

By 1984, Buell was behind bars, but young Ohio girls continued to turn up dead.

In 1989, 10-year-old Amy Mihaljevic was abducted from Bay Village. Like Debbie, she made a phone call to her mother when she was most likely already with her abductor. She resembled Krista Harrison in appearance. And even though Amy was from Bay Village and Krista was from Marshallville, two cities separated by 58 miles, Amy's body was discovered within a short drive from where police found a bloody garbage bag containing part of Krista's scalp. Like Tina, Amy's body was found in a field, on an incline, placed so that it could be easily seen from the road. Amy's body had also been stored someplace before being moved to the "dump" site. On Amy's body, the coroner discovered gold-colored fibers, but they were never compared to those gathered in the Tina Harmon and Krista Harrison homicides because Buell was already in prison when the crime occurred. Wayne County Prosecutor Martin Frantz claims his Sheriff's Department destroyed the evidence after Buell was executed, though some samples may still be kept by BCI&I.

The case of 13-year-old Barbara Barnes of Steubenville is similar, too. Barbara disappeared in December 1995, on her way to school. She was found two months later, strangled to death. But Barbara's killer went to extra lengths to hide the body, burying her in a muddy

Buell raped and tortured women inside this inconspicuous ranch home in Doylestown.

embankment in Pittsburgh. She was discovered when the river level rose with the thaw.

"I understand the circumstantial evidence could be put to Ralph Ross as well as Robert Buell," says Frantz in his office, today. The prosecutor is a gracious host and opened his files to me because he truly believes he sent the right guy to the Death House. He sees the Harrisons in public sometimes and can meet their eyes. He believes Ross, at most, is nothing more than a serial killer's apprentice.

"I know that during the investigation, Derflinger had those feelings. We ruled [Ross] out, but I can't remember how. I've always felt in my heart that Buell was guilty."

Pastor Ernie Sanders disagrees.

"Buell never killed those girls," he says. "He was by no means someone you would call a perfect citizen, but I know he didn't do it. I told him I was suspicious of his nephew, but he just kept saying that [Ross] was not smart enough to pull something like that off. You see, Buell thought he was smarter than everyone he knew. He told me that when he talked to Ralph about kidnapping women, he specifically told Ralph not to cross the line. He said not to take kids. And Ralph never argued with him, but Buell said he wasn't happy about it. A month before his execution, he told me, 'You know what? You were right all along. Ralph set me up.' And I believe him. Ralph had access to Bob's clothes and the clothes found at the crime scene were too small for Buell anymore. He'd left them for Ralph."

When I caught up with him in September 2007, Ralph Ross Jr. was living in a small house just outside Steubenville. He worked for a cable company, installing boxes. He had recently been arrested and charged with possession of marijuana.

He spoke to me on the stoop in front of his house. "I don't think Buell did it," he said. "But I don't know who did. They never questioned me about the deaths. Why would they?"

When asked why he didn't allow the detective to take his fingerprints, he became defensive. "What if something come up?" he said. "I told them if they wanted it to get a court order and take it. If they needed it, they could have got a court order."

He put his hands in his pockets and looked over the river that meanders below his house. Ross said he started talking with his uncle about kidnapping and brutalizing women when he was 13 years old and the conversations continued until Buell was caught.

"Times were different back then," he explains. "I was hanging out with my cool uncle. I thought it was just guys talking when we talked about taking those women. I should never have said anything about it to the cops. Also, he would never have gone to that softball game. Bob hated baseball." Ross, however, was a star player on his high school team. "And he was never home that summer. He was always at his girlfriend's. People called it 'Ralph's Place.'"

When asked about Krista, he abruptly ended the conversation. "I don't have anything more to say," he said. He went back inside and stood behind his screen door, glancing up and down the sidewalk. I asked him if he had anything to do with Krista's abduction and then he shut the door and disappeared into the darkness, there.

. . .

Less than a week after my newspaper article on Buell's case was published, Ross was fired from his job at the cable company in Steubenville, where he worked installing cable boxes in homes. His van was immediately emptied and driven to a location away from the main facility by unknown men, say co-workers. According to people who still work at the cable company, FBI agents have been seen at the office, questioning managers.

> "I have to question, did we miss Ralph as an accomplice? Let's pray we get an answer."

In late 2007, the FBI compared fibers taken from the body of Tina Harmon to those found on the body of Amy Mihaljevic. They do not match.

After months of requests, the Wayne County Prosecutor confirmed that all the evidence gathered in Krista's case was incinerated after Buell's execution. A detective with the Wayne County Sheriff's Office told me that Krista's case was being "re-evaluated." But prosecutor Martin Frantz says that the case will not be officially reopened. He says detectives are reviewing Tina Harmon's case, instead, to see if something further can be done there.

"I know many want to hear from Ralph Ross Jr.," writes retired detective Derflinger in an e-mail. "Why would Buell not give him up if he was involved? Was Buell worried that Ralph would talk about other cases? Do any of the departments have DNA type evidence that could link Ralph to the cases? Soooo many questions. You, I'm sure recognize the possible magnitude of this case because it ended with an execution being carried out. No one wants to be wrong and if there ever is a time not to be wrong it's with this case. I have never second guessed the outcome of the Buell case and now in my mind I have to question, did we miss Ralph as an accomplice? Let's pray we get an answer."

Hopefully, Ernie Sanders's God has grace enough to answer those prayers.

. . .

Coda:

There's a new twist to this case that has been bothering me, a co-incidence I can't wrap my head around. Do you have time for just one more strange tale?

On Wednesday, September 29, 1982, seven-year-old Dawn Marie Hendershot was abducted from Massillon, Ohio, on her way home from school. This case is no mystery. A man named Donald Maurer confessed to kidnapping her and killing her, when he became the main suspect. He actually led the police detectives to her body. He was sent to prison for the rest of his life. Of course, at the time, Buell had not yet been caught and police wondered if Maurer could have abducted Krista Harrison and Tina Harmon as well. They gave him a lie detector test, which he passed (for more information on the reliability of lie detector tests, read the chapter on Lisa Pruett's unsolved murder).

But I discovered something odd while combing through Maurer's file. Shortly before Dawn's murder, Maurer worked at a butcher shop called Salsburg Meats, in Canton, with a man named Herbert Sefert. Sefert was the same young man who found the body of Tina Harmon, while he was tracking a deer near his father's house in Bethlehem Township. Maurer knew Sefert—was hired by Sefert's brother-in-law. Could Maurer have been familiar with the Sefert's property?

It's a coincidence that calls into question everything I thought I knew about Tina's case and the evidence that authorities say links her murder to Krista's. But Maurer can't possibly be responsible for each of these murders, given the evidence that links Krista's body to Buell's home. And Maurer was in prison by the time Debbie Smith disappeared from Massillon in 1983. So, just how many serial killers were active in this small part of Ohio back then?

Is it easier to believe that a man like Sefert could have crossed paths with two separate serial killers, or that one man is responsible for both cases?

Which answer is less frightening? Which answer is more true?

Acknowledgments

Writing about grizzly murders is often a painful process for me. It hurts physically. Sometimes, my entire body tenses up and I shake all over. When I sit down in front of the computer, it's all I can do not to throw up. I'm pretty sure these are panic attacks. I get migraines, too. I have nightmares. I get depressed. Really, darkly, depressed. I can't go to the grocery store when I'm writing these stories because I look at other people in line at the register and imagine them at home torturing their kids. I start to think everyone is evil. When I get really bad, I make sure I reach out to my wife, or a parent, or a friend and ask for help bringing me back.

I was probably at my worst during the course of writing the story *The Serial Killer's Apprentice.* One night during research for that one, I found myself driving across rural Ohio, very much alone, a hundred miles from home. With what felt like my last ounce of will, I used my cell phone to call my buddy Mike.

"What's wrong?" he asked.

"Just tell me a joke, Mike," I said. "Make me laugh."

"Okay, here's one," he said. "This girl and a pedophile are walking through the woods and it's starting to get really dark, right? So the girl turns to the pedophile and says, 'Mister, I'm getting real scared.' And the pedophile looks at the girl and says, 'You think *you're* scared? I have to walk back alone.'"

There were some other people who were a little more helpful than Mike during the process of writing this book.

For Joe Kupchik's story, Fran Nagle was extremely helpful in providing information about Joe's personality and pointing me toward the people who knew Joe well. Thanks to the Kupchik family for taking the time to speak with me about Joe. Even though they do not grant many interviews, they have been quietly working behind the scenes for years to get the Cleveland Police Department to reopen Joe's case. Maybe one day the detectives will listen to what they're saying.

Garfield Heights Police Captain Robert Sackett and Detective Carl Biegacki were kind enough to share many new details about the Bev Jarosz case with me. I was inspired by their commitment to the case and hope that's apparent in the piece. Thanks also to the Jarosz family for sharing Bev's poetry with me. And thanks, Captain Sackett, for taking the time to write the foreword which precedes these stories.

Thank you, Tony Gricar, for meeting me for a beer when I popped in out of the blue to talk about your uncle. And thank you, Detective Matt Rickard for giving me the weird scoop about the science fiction novel that seems so connected to the disappearance of Ray Gricar.

"Gemini's Last Dance" could not have been written without the help of Akron Police Detectives Bertina King and Steven Null.

Detective Lieutenant Ray Arcuri of the Westlake PD invited me into his detectives' den and was extremely generous with information about the case of Tony Daniels. Thanks for that, because such a warm welcome is rare.

Retired U.S. Marshal Pete Elliott was nice enough to find some time to talk to me about Ted Conrad, the man he's hunted for nearly 40 years. Thank you. And thanks also to Kathleen Einhouse, who may have inadvertently jump-started this case again after talking to me.

Thanks again to Ted Schwarz for helping me with background information on the Lisa Pruett homicide.

I spent a couple of hours talking to Detective Christopher Bowersock during my research into the strange suicide of Joe Chandler and little of that time was actually spent talking about Joe. Thanks for sharing your stories with me. And I'd like to say thanks to Joe's friend—and executor—Mike, for helping me better understand who that man was. Also Chris Yarbrough for doing the initial research that led to Stephen Campbell.

Thanks to the families of Gina DeJesus and Mandy Berry for taking the time to talk to me at the FBI offices, and to Scott Wilson and Jennifer Meyers for setting that up.

As always, thank you to Detective Lieutenant Mark Spaetzel, for continuing to investigate Amy Mihaljevic's abduction/murder. The same goes for Special Agent Phil Torsney and Jim Larkin. I am humbled by the effort, time, and passion the three of you have devoted to this unsolved case. I know you'll solve it one day.

Thanks, Phil Trexler, for sharing your experience at the Death House on the day Robert Buell was executed. And thanks, Jack Swint, for giving me Buell's personal documents. Yeah, thanks a lot, buddy.

Special thanks to retired Cuyahoga County Coroner Dr. Elizabeth Balraj, current Coroner Dr. Frank Miller, Jim in photography, and Heather in records for putting up with my frequent requests for documents and photographs, and for providing them in a timely manner. City hall could learn a thing or two from your office about open records.

To Mike Lewis and the rest of the crew at Confidential Investigative Services, thanks for always helping me track down killers or fugitives at a moment's notice.

To Frank Lewis, my editor at the *Free Times* and now *Cleveland Scene*: thank you for letting me go on wild adventures on the clock, for editing many of these stories for the paper, and for re-editing them for this book. And thanks to art director Ron Kretsch of *Free Times*, and now *Cleveland Scene*, for help with photos.

A thank you to David Gray and his hard-working gang at Gray & Company— Chris Andrikanich, Jane Lassar, Frank Lavallo, Rob Lucas, and Jane Wipper—for helping me put this book together and getting me out to talk about these cases. Thanks to Laura Peppers for her talents as a copyeditor and Pat Fernberg for proofreading. And thanks to David Marburger for his attention to detail and care for the First Amendment.

Extra special thanks to my wife, Julie, for listening to me go on and on about each of these unsolved cases and for humoring me every time I was convinced I had solved one.

The following is an excerpt from
James Renner's book:

AMY

MY SEARCH FOR HER KILLER

CHAPTER ONE

Taken

I FELL IN LOVE with Amy Mihaljevic not long before her body was discovered lying facedown in an Ashland County wheat field. I fell for her the first time I saw that school photo Northeast Ohio TV stations flashed at the beginning of every newscast in the weeks following her kidnapping in the autumn of 1989—the photo with the side-saddle ponytail. First love in the heart of an eleven-year-old boy is consuming. One look at that brown-eyed girl and I knew that, if she had gone to my school, she would have been the one I passed notes to behind Miss Kline's back.

But Amy didn't go to my school. She went to Bay Middle, which was somewhere on another planet, far from the sub-suburban cow town where I lived with my father. I had a vague notion, though, that Bay Village was somewhere near my mother's apartment in Rocky River. When I visited Mom every other weekend, I looked for Amy's face in the crowds at Westgate Mall, hoping to find her wandering the aisles at Waldenbooks—as if she'd simply been lost there the whole time. I would be the one to lead her home.

Throughout the last part of October and the whole of November 1989, local newscasts began their six o'clock coverage with updates on the investigation. It was my routine to come home from school and turn on the TV to see if there were any new developments, to see if she'd finally been found. I watched closely. I learned to pronounce that difficult last name—"Mah-*hal*-leh-vick." I memorized the face of her abductor from the police-artist sketches and searched for him in crowds.

With time, the reports became less frequent. A brief news segment in December covered her eleventh birthday party, which her family celebrated without her. Then the reports dropped off altogether. But I knew she was alive. She had to be. I was supposed to meet the girl in that photo. Maybe at a high-school football game five years in the future. Or in college. She would be found, and I would get to tell her that I never stopped looking for her.

On Thursday, February 8, 1990, I came home and flipped on the television. I sat cross-legged in front of it, and when the tube finally warmed up, her face was on the screen. It was that fifth-grade class picture again. I turned the volume up and listened as my innocence died.

Dead.

Murdered.

Dumped.

The news anchors cut to aerial pictures of County Road 1181 in Ashland County. Men in dark trench coats milled about a wheat field, tiny black specs in a sea of brown. The image was strangely corporeal, like the final glimpse of earth seen by a detached soul. It was here, they said, that Amy's body had been found. A jogger had spotted what looked like a large doll lying on the frozen ground during a morning run. That patch of road they kept showing looked as far from the civilized cul-de-sacs of Bay Village as anyone could get. I didn't see a single house in the background. Just a ragged field stretching to the horizon. It looked desolate. It looked unkind.

Police and FBI were guarded with information, but there were some details. We learned Amy was stabbed in the neck and hit on the head with a blunt instrument. No word on time of death. She was found fully clothed, but no one was sure what exactly that meant, yet. The composite sketches of her abductor appeared again, under an urgent voice-over. The news anchor couldn't stress one fact enough—further tests were being conducted to determine if she had been sexually assaulted.

I swallowed the information like a diluted poison, feeling it burn away a kind of protective inner coating that had once made me feel safe. Years later, when I tried my first cigarette at Seven Ranges Boy Scout Camp, I would remember this feeling—like healthy tissue being singed by flames. Still, I couldn't stop listening to the details. I couldn't stop the words from forming scenarios in my head—silent films that obeyed all the new facts and ended with Amy's body in that field.

I would not be the one who would find her and bring her back to her mother. That was a fantasy I could no longer indulge. Sitting there, staring into the smiling eyes of a girl now dead, I began to entertain a different dream. Adrenaline lit up my senses, making them detailed and fine. Now I pictured myself tracking down her killer, following him back to his lair. I saw myself knocking on his door, a snub-nosed revolver tucked under the waistband of my raggedy jeans. When he answered, I filled him with hot lead. I'd become an eleven-year-old vigilante. . . .

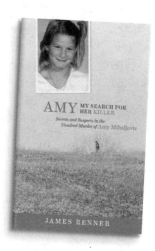

Available in Bookstores.